History

of the

Red River Valley Conference

of the

Augustana Lutheran Church

by

J. Edor Larson

"We have heard with our ears, O
God, our fathers have told us, what
work thou didst in their days, in the
times of old." — Ps. 44:1.

Published by the Red River Valley Conference
1953

Printed in
Lutheran Publishing House
Blair, Nebraska

FOREWORD

In retrospect as we review the birth and growth of the Red River Valley Conference, the Doxology, our most Christian hymn, comes to our mind. For the past forty years the congregations of the Conference have had evidences of "his lovingkindness and tender mercies." Thanksgiving and praise to God should be the spontaneous response of all those who are privileged to read and study this brief history of the Red River Valley Conference.

This thankful spirit is not dependent upon outward circumstances alone. For the history of our Conference indicates moments of deep anxiety and concern. Rural areas plagued with drought, crop failures, floods, windstorms and hail. Some of the winters of the past have been described as fit only for "Scandinavians and other fur-bearing animals." And the condition of the world in general the past forty years has not been a time for thanksgiving. "We are troubled on every side," and we are distressed; we are perplexed, but not unto despair; we are cast down, though not completely destroyed. This in certain respects is inevitable, for does not Paul in his genealogy of hope as we have it in Romans, state: "We also rejoice in our tribulations; knowing that tribulation worketh steadfastness; and steadfastness, approvedness; and approvedness, hope; and hope putteth not to shame; because the love of God hath been shed abroad in our hearts through the Holy Spirit which was given unto us."

The 17,143 confirmed members in the 112 congregations of the Red River Valley Conference have more than outward circumstances to give for an explanation to their singing of the Doxology today. Through the faithful preaching of the Word of God and the administering of the Sacraments there are those who have "passed from death unto life," who have acquired "unsearchable riches in Christ Jesus," who have become "new creatures" and now confess "for me to live is Christ."

If in the reading of this history our souls are still steeped in anxiety, and beset with fear, let us try to recall the spirit of those pioneers of our Conference who were gloriously radiant in spite of supreme denials and sufferings. Think of the growth and the extension of the church through the missionary activity of the pioneer pastors who served as itinerants to six, to eight, to as many as twelve congregations. Our pioneer pastirs, serving in the Red River Valley Conference, would have been the most miserable of men had they counted their compensations, satisfactions or triumphs solely on outward circumstances. The formula of joy and peace in the service of the church is not found therein, but in the inner witness of the Lord's gracious approval, "Well done, good and faithful servant."

It was at the Elim Lutheran Church, Fargo, North Dakota, that it was voted "that the Conference begin to function immediately following the next meeting of the Minnesota Conference, if said Conference grants our petition for the formation of a new conference and recommends it to Synod." Favorable action was taken by the Augustana Lutheran Church on this petition, for in 1913 when the Red River Valley Conference met for its first annual convention there were ninety congregations reporting a membership of 6,865. Twenty years later the Conference consisted of ninety-six congregations and 10,230 confirmed members, or a gain of forty-nine per cent during twenty years. As of today our membership stands at 17,143 confirmed members in 112 congregations. It was in 1941 that the 23 congregations in the Bismarck and Sheyenne Districts of North Dakota, with a total confirmed membership of 2,347, were given to the Red River Valley Conference by the Minnesota Conference.

What will the history of the Red River Valley Conference as here presented mean for the member of the local church? What can the church member do to help share in carrying out the Great Commission? What part will we have in helping to write history in the Red River Valley Conference the next forty years? Our concern must be all-inclusive, "All must go and go to all." The world situation is urgent and will brook no delay. In the sphere of our local congregations we will want to know the fellowship of His sufferings; by God's grace we will want to be instruments in that Kingdom where His will is done. That life that God has given to us in Christ, will not be hoarded by those who possess it, but it will be given for the life of the world. The Great Commission is still possible because the crucified and risen Christ speaks, "I am with you always."

Walter E. Carlson,
President of the R.R.V. Conference.

GREETING

Many interesting historical facts regarding the initiation and development of our Christian work have undoubtedly been lost. The men and women who lived and labored in the early days have passed on, often leaving no written records of their part in establishing churches and institutions. What they narrated in moments of reminiscence was soon forgotten by younger people with whom they shared their experiences.

Our Augustana Church is keenly concerned today about preserving records still extant, letters written by Church leaders, old periodicals and photographs. The Red River Valley Conference has been alert to this need and has selected an historian to be primarily responsible for preserving the chronicles of the Conference. It has been his task also to commit some of the most important facts to writing. The present volume will be welcomed, not only by members of the Conference but by all members and friends of our Church everywhere. Down through the decades, this compendium of Red River annals will help both to inform and to inspire future generations of pastors and laymen.

Painstaking study of available sources has gone into the writing of this book. Pastor Larson has been eager to present an accurate record and yet with a proper sense of dramatic values. This assures the reader of both pleasure and profit as he peruses this important contribution to the historical record of Augustana.

Oscar A. Benson,
President of the Augustana Lutheran Church.

GREETING

History is a record of the past: a reflector of the future. Our knowledge of the years that have gone, gives direction to that which lies ahead.

It is with a feeling of thanksgiving that we welcome the publication of the History of The Red River Valley Conference. The Conference and its Executive Board have taken action several times to have this history published, but now it has become a reality.

To those who have been privileged to share in the development of the Christian Church, it is a satisfaction to learn that some of the evidences of God's work among the Lutherans who pioneered in this area, are to be preserved. While it is impossible to record all the experiences of "the heroes of faith" who began and developed our Lutheran Church in Northwestern Minnesota and Dakota, this will reveal many of God's marvelous dealings toward them.

The Lord has never failed us. He has led through privations to plenty, from small beginnings to well established churches. The Saviour, Who has been with His people in ages past, will be present to help in days to come. In Him the work of the Church remains secure, and through Him coming generations also will gain the victory.

Oscar O. Gustafson,
President of Red River Valley Conference 1922-1952.

PREFACE

It was with a great deal of trepidation that the undersigned took the assignment of attempting to write the History of the Red River Valley Conference. Even though I have spent twenty-two years of my ministry within the territory in question—thirteen of these within this Conference—my knowledge of its history is woefully limited. Even where I have had sources to consult I have failed in that I possess neither the eagle eye of an historian nor the pen of a ready writer. In addition I have carried on the regular pastoral work in my parish.

In spite of all this I promised to accept the assignment. It has been a work of pleasure. It has been intensely interesting to read the historical accounts of individual congregations, to scan the Minutes of the Synod, Conferences and Districts, and to peruse the often faded pages of the church press from years ago.

We regret that we must limit ourselves as to the material. We would like to include a brief history of each congregation but that would make the volume too large. As the reader will notice we have included what we consider "key positions" in the various sections of the Conference.

There are many to whom I feel indebted for help and encouragement—the Executive Committee of the Conference, the Publication Committee, pastors and lay people. Among the latter we want to mention Miss Mabel Olson, Bismarck, who has kindly examined a portion of the manuscript and offered valuable suggestions. A special thanks to the people of the Parkers Prairie parish for their tolerance. The work has been done during spare moments snatched from the regular routine work in the parish and a few days taken from vacation time.

Undoubtedly there are mistakes and misstatements as well as omissions. For these we ask pardon. We do honor our pioneers and later generations who have built our Conference and we glorify God in Christ that we may have His Kingdom in our midst.

J. Edor Larson.

CONTENTS

I. THE RED RIVER VALLEY
The Nile of the North

Geographers tell us that the Red River Valley is the center of America, equally distant from the Arctic, Atlantic and Pacific Oceans and the Gulf of Mexico.[1] Geologists claim that the rich soil of this region was formed by the waters of Lake Agazzis which at one time, in the distant past, covered the entire area. They have dug up clamshells fifteen hundred miles away from any ocean. Botanists have discovered one hundred and twenty-five different grasses and two thousand varieties of flowering plants.[2] Historians have much to relate. They point out that the Indians knew the riches of the Valley, wherefore they detoured the explorers to the north and to the south. Consequently this region was not discovered by white man until quite late. Nevertheless, the country was the envy of the Indians as well as the French and English fur traders. When the Revolutionary War was raging in the eastern section of our country the struggle for survival and conquest was being fought in the Valley.[3] Even Napoleon had his eye upon the Red River Valley, but decided to conquer Russia first, and that military expedition changed his plans.[4] Thomas Jefferson read Mackenzie's book on this section of America and the result was the Louisiana Purchase, including all lands drained by the Mississippi River. Historians assert that the first colonists to settle and build the cities of St. Paul, Minneapolis and Stillwater, Minnesota, came from the north.[5] The early explorers wrote: "There is perhaps no finer country in the world for the residence of uncivilized man than that which occupies the space between the Red River and Lake Superior. It abounds in everything necessary to the wants and comforts of such a people. Fish, venison and fowl, with wild rice, are in a great plenty; while at the same time their subsistence requires that bodily exercise so necessary to health and vigor."[6] And some of those who read this description knew many "uncivilized" men for whom the Valley would be a Paradise. There were many who tried this new and rich country.

The Vikings

From times immemorial the people of Sweden have been adventurers. The story of the Vikings is singular in the history of the world. Not only did they skirt the coast of Europe from Spitsbergen to Sicily, but they pointed their dragon-headed ships westward across the great Atlantic and landed on the American shores—perhaps a hundred years before Columbus. According to the Kensington Stone, discovered by Olof Ohman near the village of Kensington, Minnesota, in 1890, "eight Swedes and twenty-two Norwegians, on exploration," penetrated into this section of the country as early as 1362. Not only has the Runestone been recognized as being of greatest importance, but iron tools dating back to that early date bear additional testimony. Thus a battle-ax was found under two feet of unplowed prairie near Climax, Minnesota; another was discovered resting underground in the roots of an old oak tree near Alexandria; a third lay under eighteen inches of soil near Madison, Wisconsin; while a fourth had found its way to an Iowa Falls museum. They are all similar in design and workmanship. They are not of Indian origin, as "the Indians never worked in iron."[7] What happened to these early adventurers—if they were here—we do not know.

References

[1] Kelsey, Vera, Red River Runs North, p. 1. By permission.
[2] Ibid, p. 14.
[3] Ibid, p. 63.
"Some fur traders had described the Red River Valley as a desert. Was it true? Or had they spread such reports in order to keep the people out?" (Building Minnesota. By Theo. Blegen. D. C. Heath & Company. 1938, p. 89. By permission.)
[4] Kelsey, Vera, Red River Runs North, p. 67.
[5] Ibid, p. 15.
[6] Ibid, p. 67.
[7] Minneapolis Tribune, July 8, 1951.
For a complete discussion and description of the Kensington Stone, see "History of Douglas and Grant Counties, Minnesota." Constant Larson, Editor-in-chief, p. 72 ff.

II. THE BEGINNINGS

From Early Days

From this dim and distant past we go forward five centuries, when Swedish voices again echoed across the lakes and in the forests primeval. The first Swedish settler in Minnesota is said to have been John Fahlstrom. He came with the Hudson Bay Company before 1819. He later married an Indian woman, was converted and became a Methodist missionary among the Indians.[1]

It seems quite evident that a great deal of effort was made on the part of the early immigrants to induce their relatives and friends in Sweden to join them in this country. The National House of Representatives heard Ignatius Donelly say so eloquently in 1864: "With nearly a billion (acres) of unsettled land on one side of the Atlantic and with many millions of poor and oppressed people on the other, let them (the people of the North) organize the exodus which must come, and build, if necessary, a bridge of gold across the chasm which divides them, that the chosen races of mankind may occupy the chosen land of the earth."[2] We are told that between 1850 and 1880 the population of the land grew to be four times as large, but the membership in the churches increased twelve times.[3]

Some of the early immigrants described the land of their adoption as one of "milk and honey." *Jönköpimgsbladet*, May 26, 1846—according to George M. Stephenson—quotes a beggar girl who in turn quoted letters from America, which painted the new world in "far more attractive colors than Joshua's returned spies portrayed the promised land to the children of Israel." "In America," so the girl reported, "the hogs eat their fill of raisins and dates that grow everywhere, and when they are thirsty they drink from ditches flowing with wine."[4] It seems that the imagination in conjunction with zeal carried some of the pioneers quite far from the golden truth. Thus

13

later Peter Cassel writes, "that even the thunder in Sweden sounded like the report of a pistol shot compared with the heavy artillery of the heavens in America,"[5] or where he declares that the "cornfields are more like woods than grain fields," or again when he goes on to say that "there are no beggars here, I have yet to see a lock on a door. . . . I never heard of theft."[6]

A newspaper editor in Kansas frightened his readers with the story of ice and snow in Minnesota, adding that if the people there would not starve to death they would surely perish from the cold. But from the North came but words of sympathy for the "miserable denizens of the torrid zone."[7] In 1869 the Board of Immigration sent a Norwegian journalist, Paul Hjelm Hanson, on a trip from Alexandria to the Red River, that he later would prepare a series of letters about western Minnesota to be published in newspapers in Scandinavia. He left Alexandria by oxcart July 12, 1869, on a real "pioneer journey." He did not only blaze the way for Scandinavian settlers in the Red River Valley, but he also wrote: "I have gotten rid of my rheumatism and instead I have gained much strength and good humor."[8]

It required both strength and humor to face the arduous tasks of pioneering. An early pastor reports: "As yet the 'horned horses' are generally used, after which I have had the pleasure to ride to and from the church (Clarissa). As every man knows, these animals are driven by commands, which must be very loud and be impressed by means of a sturdy pole. But it goes across corduroy roads, stumps and logs, and one needs to be put together well not to be shaken to pieces and one must have strong nerves so as not to lose equilibrium. Once in a while you come to a stop because the turn in the road is too sharp and the vehicle bumps against a large tree."[9]

In an age of perfected mechanization it is interesting and challenging to read, that A. F. Sjostrom brought an old English hoe with him as the only tool with which to till the soil and also an ax to use in clearing the land. He made his first drag with pegs, all of wood; grain was seeded by hand, cut with scythe or cradle, tied with straw and threshed with flail. A trip to market with oxen took two days.

And the beginnings of the church were equally primitive. "The church was built of oak, tamarack and basswood. Each land owner was to deliver two hundred feet of logs at the Pelican Rapids saw mill. Gustav Young drew plans and was foreman. The working day was seven a.m. to six p.m. Each day began and closed with prayer." [10]

It was to this kind of life that the early immigrants were invited. "Last fall," reports Pastor P. Sjöblom, in 1882, "this State sent a large number of agents to Sweden to bring people over here and because of the hard times over there we expect a large immigration next summer." [11]

The First Settlement

In the year 1863 seventeen men started out from Red Wing, Minnesota, traveling in a northwesterly direction. After a most tiresome and tedious journey they came to Glenwood. Sixteen of the men were so discouraged and tired that they turned back. One of them, Olof Fahlin, continued and came to Oscar Lake where he filed on a homestead and established his home on the southern shore, a short distance from what is now Holmes City. He brought his family the following year. Thus began the first Swedish Lutheran colony in that section of Minnesota which is now a part of the Red River Valley Conference. The Kensington adventurers, who had come by way of Hudson Bay, Nelson River, across Lake Winnipeg and up the Red River, had in times of distress chanted "Ave Maria", but the colonists of more modern times were the spiritual product of the Reformation and the children of great religious revivals in Sweden. Therefore, they brought their Bibles, Luther's Catechism, and a good variety of sound books of sermons and other devotional literature, including in most cases

Luther's Church Postil. They were much concerned about their spiritual life.

God was also mindful of the spiritual needs of His people in the dispersion. In 1865 Pastors Eric Norelius and Peter Carlson traveled through these regions on foot and by oxcart.[12] The following year the special attention of the Minnesota Conference was called to the "dispersed countrymen who are scattered almost all over the whole State of Minnesota." A committee was therefore elected to engage a traveling missionary. Mr. Jonas Magney, a student, was secured and he brought the gospel message to the people in these settlements. The initial result of the efforts and leadership of this home missionary was the organization of the first congregation of the present Red River Valley Conference—Oscar Lake. The organization took place in the Olof Fahlin home, August 8, 1866. We are told that the secretary at the meeting used an immigrant trunk as his writing desk and seats "for the audience were the joists of the incomplete floor." The charter members were: Mr. and Mrs. Olof Fahlin (Falin), Ola Paulson, John Olson Fahlin, Mr. and Mrs. Jon Mattson, Mr. and Mrs. Christoffer Person, Carl Alfred Peterson, Mr. and Mrs. Isak Peterson, and Gustaf Johnson. Others joined the following year. According to the Church Records the first deacons were elected in 1867 and were: Christoffer Person, L. J. Dalen, J. N. Nedstrom. Trustees were: Olof Paulson, Olof Fahlin, Peter Peterson.

The first church building was twenty-four by thirty feet and twelve feet high. It was located on a hill on the Olof Fahlin homestead, one mile north and one mile west of the Oscar Lake church.[13]

The country was then in its virgin state with Indians roaming the country. It is reported that Mr. Fahlin could at times count up to forty canoes on Oscar Lake. The Indians were on the whole very friendly to the white settlers. The colonists hailed to a large extent from the northern part of Sweden,

Dr. Oscar A. Benson, President Augustana
Lutheran Church

Pastor Walter E. Carlson
President R. R. V. Conference
1952-

Dr. Oscar O. Gustafson
President R. R. V. Conference
1922-1952

especially Härjedalen. An editorial declares that "the early Swedish colonists who came to Minnesota lived first in Illinois and other states, but they yearned for the north, where they expected to find climatic conditions corresponding more to those in Sweden. They loved the fresh air, the high blue sky, the long twilight, the regularity of the seasons, the steady winter, the clear, fresh water, the crystal-clear lakes and the variations in nature." [14]

The Oscar Lake congregation was admitted into the Augustana Synod at its convention in Berlin (now Swedona), Illinois, June 13-18, 1867. It numbered at that time fify-seven communicants and four children. Naturally it was not easy to procure pastoral care for this frontier congregation and for neighboring communities. The Conference asked Pastor J. S. Nilson of Watertown, Minnesota, to visit the field. Later on appeals were made to the Synod for a traveling missionary, but the only immediate result was a visit by Pastor Theodore Dahl, who had his field in Meeker County. In 1868 the Minnesota Conference assigned a lay worker, F. Westerdahl, to serve Holmes City. The next year Pastor J. P. Lundblad, who was then serving New London, was urged to visit the field.[15] By Conference decision Pastors P. Beckman and T. H. Dahl visited Oscar Lake, Lake Ida and Crooked Lake.[16]

An Early Missionary

Jonas Magney was ordained in June 1870 on a call to become assistant to Pastor Eric Norelius in Vasa, Minnesota. The summer of the same year Pastor Magney was sent on a home missionary journey. His report gives us a most graphic description of the experiences and vicissitudes of a pioneer missionary. We give therefore his report in full, translated by Dr. Emeroy Johnson from the Swedish, as published in the Missionären":

"Since I made an extended mission journey in the area of

17

the Conference last summer, I wish to give a brief account thereof.

"The region which I visited was Stearns, Todd, Douglas, Pope and Otter Tail Counties. Since it was out of the question to secure anyone to drive for me so far west, and since there are no railroads or other means of transportation available, I got a horse and buggy, and thus equipped I set out on the first of August to Chisago Lake where I attended business matters. (Chisago Lake was Magney's home.)

"After a week there I left on a Thursday morning and after a trip of three days, covering a distance of about one hundred and sixty miles, I was at a place some ten or fifteen miles north of Sauk Center, at a sawmill which now is also a flourmill, in the neighborhood of a Swedish settlement.

"Sunday morning was somewhat rainy, and since I could not go any further with my horse on account of lack of roads, I left the horse at the sawmill and went on foot to look for the Swedes who had settled a few miles from there. However, before I reached the settlement I met a Norwegian who was on his way to a Norwegian settlement a few miles north of the sawmill. He persuaded me to go with him and preach in his stead in the forenoon. In the meantime a message was sent to the Swedish settlement so I could meet with them in the afternoon, and then I had the pleasure of seeing about twenty persons gathered.

"On Monday forenoon we had another meeting and celebrated holy communion. I visited this settlement three times and had five meetings there. There were about fourteen families, most of them from Skane. When I visited them on the way home a congregation was organized there called 'Askeryd.'

"In the forenoon I drove twenty miles northeast from Moore's Mill to a place called Swan Lake, in Todd county. Arriving late in the evening I could not look for any Swedes that day, but stayed with an American. The following morning I met a Swedish young man and learned from him that nine claims around there had been taken by Swedes, but that all the settlers except three were away working. Therefore I could not do anything, so I returned immediately to Sauk Center, a distance of thirty or forty miles, arriving at dusk at the home of a Norwegian by the name of Jensen. A message was sent at once to some Norwegians who live in that vicinity, that at their request they had the opportunity that same evening to come together around the Word of God and the sacrament table.

"The following morning I was ready at an early hour to resume my journey, to reach Oscar Lake that day, if possible. Late in the evening I had the pleasure to meet old friends in this rather much discussed Oscar Lake settlement. I would have needed to rest the remaining three days of the week, but used them nevertheless to visit the countrymen living around there, and on Friday forenoon I had services in a Swedish settlement known by the name of Prairie settlement or Norunga congregation. In the afternoon of the same day we had services at a place fourteen miles from there at Red Rock Lake. Prairie settlement is only eight miles south of Oscar Lake and will presumably join with that congregation in calling a pastor. Here they insisted that a congregation had been organized, but when I saw the minutes I found that the whole affair was merely a meeting of the settlers at which they had agreed to organize a congregation by the name of Norunga. No constitution had been adopted and no one had signed the membership list. Therefore, in consultation with them I set a date for a meeting at which a congregation was organized and a constitution adopted. They also decided to get materials for a church that winter, and according to resolution then adopted it would be thirty feet wide and thirty-two feet long. How large the congregation is at present I do not remember; but they had hopes that there soon would be one hundred communicants. I visited this settlement six times and found not

19

only the ordinary churchly spirit, but also in not a few instances a true Christian spirit.

"On Sunday, August 14, I preached the Word of God twice to the people at Oscar Lake, where they were gathered in their church which consists of log walls under a shingle roof of rough boards with only a few windows. The next day I drove through Alexandria to Crooked Lake, a settlement lying six to twelve miles southeast of Alexandria. Here I preached to a large number of Swedes on Tuesday and Wednesday, gave communion and baptized seven children, of whom three were from the same family. A great hunger for the Word of God was evident among these people. In the first house that I visited I was met by a woman who, according to the testimony of others and according to what I myself learned later, was a spiritually minded woman from Dalarna. She met me with tears in her eyes and with the words, 'God still hears prayer.' I preached four times in this settlement, which consists of forty families; and enjoyed a pleasant stay with these serious-minded people.

"On Wednesday evening I had a service for quite a few Scandinavians in Alexandria. There are no Swedes residing in this place permanently, but those who are there need all the Word of God they can get. Early on Thursday morning I drove to the Lake Ida settlement situated six to twelve miles north of Alexandria, where I had services in the afternoon of the same day, and also on Friday forenoon, at which time we had the Lord's Supper, and several children were baptized. About four o'clock in the afternoon I set out on a journey of some twenty miles to a settlement known by the name of Parkers Prairie, situated in the southeastern part of Otter Tail County. Here I found old friends from Chisago Lake. Had holy communion with full service on Sunday forenoon; in the afternoon baptism of children and an hour Bible study. Here about twenty claims have been taken by Swedes and there is room for many more, who will be welcome on condition that they are churchly. No pastor had visited them before this.

"On Monday morning I was ready to set out towards the West through Otter Tail County, to visit these regions which are so unknown to us, but a heavy and continuous rain prevented me, and I had to be content to remain still that day. On Tuesday morning I was going to get started at last, but the roads were exceptionally wet, and my horse had been injured in one of his front legs, so that it was with difficulty I covered twenty miles that day, and just as evening was coming on I came to the home of a Swede living three miles from a place called Chippewa.* I could not get lodging there, however, but was told to go to the next house, where a light still was shining in the window, and where an American, a single man, was living. I was well received there and allowed to share whatever there was in the house. I was permitted to let my horse go in the pasture, and I had to stay while I got some medicine for his injured leg before I dared to continue on my journey on roads which were still muddier after the previous night's rain. During the time I was delayed here, about a day and a half, I used the opportunity to find some six or seven families living a couple of miles away. I preached one sermon there and baptized two children.

"About noon on Thursday I started out with my horse at a slow walk towards Evansville, ten miles away. Here I stayed with a Swede by the name of Dahlheim from Stockholm, who showed me every kindness. He said it would be impossible to gather the countrymen there just on a moment's notice, but that it would be best to put up some notices along the public road, announcing services for some future day. I followed this advice, and after I had gotten the housewife to wash some of the most necessary clothes for me and I had written some posters, which the man promised to put up, I set out on my journey to Oscar Lake, where I had announced services for Saturday, and also a business meeting of the congregation and a meeting with some children who wanted to be enrolled for

---

* Is now Brandon.

confirmation. However, on Friday evening I had service and holy communion for some families living between Evansville and Oscar Lake. Evansville lies at the northern border of Douglas county. About thirty Swedish families live there.

"On Saturday I was up at dawn to continue the journey to Oscar Lake, in order to get there by one o'clock, the hour set for the above mentioned meeting. But I lost my way and did not arrive until four o'clock. Fortunately the settlers had followed an old habit of coming late, so I found the people gathered. The next day, Sunday, August 28, I had holy communion with full service at Oscar Lake in the forenoon. In the afternoon I had communion service in Norunga, and Monday I had service and congregational meeting.

"Now it was time for me to think of turning homewards, to attend the Conference meeting in St. Paul and church dedication in Vasa, but circumstances led me to make different plans. For one thing my horse was unable to walk as much as would be necessary to bring me to the Conference in time, and for another thing my journey had revealed such a great need for more work among the countrymen out here. I was concerned especially about what to do with the many young people who wanted to be confirmed, some of whom were past the usual confirmation age. Therefore, I decided to stay and do what I could for them.

"The first problem was how to get them together in a hurry, and how to arrange for them to get their sustenance at some place during the time needed for their instruction. Most of the children lived at Oscar Lake and that was the only place we could meet. I presented the matter to the people, appealing to them to open their homes to the children who had to come from a distance. Six responded immediately that each of them would take care of one child during that time. Now I sent notice to those who had asked for confirmation, and I traveled fifty miles to get to them all together. In this way I succeeded

22

in getting twenty children from six settlements. Fourteen children were from Oscar Lake, one from Norunga, one from Parkers Prairie, Otter Tail County, one from Sauk Center, two from Crooked Lake, and two from Lake Ida. I met with these fourteen days within a period of six weeks, and had the pleasure of finding them quite willing to study.

"During this time I visited the different settlements. I was up in Otter Tail County twice, once over to the eastern part and once to the western part, also visiting Evansville, where I had a communion service. In the western part of Otter Tail County there was not much that could be done, except that I got some information as to where there are prospects for settlements and for churchly homes. Most of the Swedish settlers were single men who now were out working. I found two places, however—Eagle Lake and Fergus Falls—which soon will require attention. At one of these places it was said that about thirty claims had been taken by Swedes. Otter Tail is settled almost exclusively by Norwegians, and the Swedes there are quite intermingled. But I heard of Swedes one hundred and fifty miles farther on from where I was, and if I had had time I surely would have gone to visit them.

"Besides these journeys I worked to get the church in Oscar Lake ready so that they could use it in cold weather. At the above mentioned congregational meeting it was decided that the debt on the church building should be paid this fall, and to get the money needed for this each communicant was taxed fifty cents. A freewill subscription was begun for the finishing of the church interior and for the purchase of a stove. Everything that is to be bought is rather expensive out here and cash is hard to get. This makes the prospect somewhat gloomy at present; but I found a way; I drove to Alexandria, twenty miles from the settlement, and secured a promise that wheat would be accepted for anything that the church would need. Now the people were in the midst of threshing, and I grasped the opportunity to be along and shake the harvest tree.

A subscription was begun and both enemies and friends were visited. Seventy bushels of wheat and thirty dollars in money were collected, the work was completed, all to everyone's satisfaction. As far as I could understand the church was ready, when I left, to the extent that they could use it on cold days, and something had also been done to improve its appearance. If the people continue as they have begun, they will assuredly have the church completely ready this winter. Naturally I spent more time at this place than any other.

"On October 16 I had confirmation, and it was surprising to see the number of people who attended. During the following week I made a tour of the settlements, except Evansville which I had visited three times previously. I conducted communion services and attended to whatever other pastoral duties were necessary. Not until the 24th of October, the day after the Nineteenth Sunday after Trinity, did I set out on the journey home. I did not take the same route as when I went out, but went by way of Monongalia, Kandiyohi, Meeker, Wright and Carver counties, and had the pleasure of meeting brethren and friends.

"After having traveled about thirteen hundred miles in three months with my horse, preached fifty or sixty times, baptized forty-eight children and confirmed twenty, I was glad to reach my beloved home on November 5.

"May the Lord bless the sowing of His Word unto the salvation of many souls." [17]

White Unto Harvest

That the Lord of the harvest was blessing the sowing of His eternal Word is evident from the fact that eight congregations were organized by Pastor Magney during the year 1871. Six of these were within what is now the Alexandria District, viz. Norunga, May 26; Fahlun, May 31; Christine Lake, July 24; Eagle Lake, October 17; Parkers Prairie, October 23; Wennersborg, "Fall of 1871." The congregation at Lake Ida (Carfield) had been organized in 1869. We are, therefore, as it were, brought back to Apostolic times and the missionary journeys of St. Paul in Asia Minor. Thus the Kingdom of God was being established among the early settlers. The work of organizing congregations continued. The Central Swede Grove was organized in 1874, Lekvatten (Holmes City) in 1875; Spruce Hill, in 1876; Svea (Calvary), Alexandria; Fridhem, Barrett; Augustana, Elizabeth; and Augustana, Fergus Falls, all in 1877; Amor (Zion), 1878.

The colonization naturally followed the railroads. "The steam engines that took the settlers into the heart of America could equally well carry the ministers of Christ; and all denominations were busy organizing congregations in the towns and farming centers that grew up along the railroad lines." [18] About this time the Northern Pacific railroad had been completed northward and the pioneers pressed on where there were transportation facilities. Thus in 1871 two congregations were organized north of the above mentioned section—at Upsala and Eksjo, near Detroit Lakes. These congregations were served by traveling missionaries, principally Jonas Magney. In 1872 he spent seven months in this work while he was pastor in Cannon Falls, Minnesota. There were also others who labored in these fields. The diary of Pastor Magney contains this interesting item: "If brother Cavallin wishes to revive old memories then I might tell him in passing that this settlement (Little Sauk) is precisely the one he visited with me in 1871, when I sang so devoutly while we were waiting for the worshipers who were hindered from coming because of rain; and he expressed his impatience with me because of my phlegmatic waiting." [19]

In 1873 the Minnesota Conference reported to the Synod that it had three main mission fields:

1. "Along the Pacific railroad, from Lake Superior in the East to the Red River in the West—yes, even to the Mis-

souri, since new settlements arise along the railroad as it is extended westward. On many of these fields there is a genuine spiritual interest and inquiry for the Word of God. On the other hand there is also a deep darkness and indifference."

2. "Along the St. Paul and Pacific railroad in the northwestern part of Minnesota. There are already ten organized congregations, all vacant. There are an estimated 5,000 souls on this field.

3. "The field southwest along the St. Paul and Sioux City railroad.

"Even with the best will and greatest efforts the Conference has been unable to meet adequately the crying needs." [20]

The Synodical Mission Board reported: "The only way, almost, in which it has been possible to carry on home mission work, has been to persuade pastors—the congregations giving their consent—to travel for a few months, breaking the Bread of Life among the many spiritually unfortunate countrymen." [21] "From all directions," reports the Conference President, P. Sjoblom, to the Synod, "we hear spiritual distress calls, 'Come over and help us.' It is painful to have to answer their cries with: 'We have no one to send.' Because of the winds of refreshing which have swept almost our entire Conference, these petitions for help have been more intense than ever." The very same report mentions that Pastors N. J. Brink, L. A. Hocanzon, J. Magney, and S. J. Kronberg "have spent a few months in the service of the home mission and have been supported from the Mission Treasury." [22]

That the burden of the cause of the church among the countrymen weighed heavily upon the hearts of the leaders and the pastors is easily discerned from the official reports and from correspondence in the church press. Thus the President of the Synod says: "To have eight or ten places, far apart, to visit and to have no way of travel except by horses or on foot, to have to be out in all kinds of weather, to live wherever you happen to be, to preach almost daily without the opportunity of preparation—these are some of the difficulties our pastors encounter." Or again: "Where a pastor baptizes, in a single year, seventy children whose parents do not belong to any church or another pastor reports that out of sixty-four baptisms only fourteen had parents who were church members; and when often more than half of the confirmands came from non-church members—we have a situation which ought not to continue." [23]

References

[1] Svenskarna i Amerika, I, p. 266.
  Norelius, T. A. In Minneapolis Tribune, Sunday, July 6, 1952.
[2] Blegen, Theo., Historical Society Bulletin, 1926. Minnesota's Campaign for Immigrants, p. 5.
[3] Ibid, p. 5.
[4] Svenskarna i Amerika, I, p. 238.
[5] Ibid, p. 239.
[6] Ibid, p. 240.
[7] Minnesota Historical Society Bulletin.
[8] Ibid, p. 8.
[9] Skaffaren, September 10, 1890, J. Magney.
[10] History of Swede Grove Lutheran Church, Pelican Rapids, Minnesota.
[11] Minutes, Minnesota Conference, 1882, p. 7.
[12] Minutes Red River Valley Conference, 1915, p. 11; 1931, p. 11.
[13] Johnson, Emeroy, A Church Planted, p. 287.
[14] Skaffaren, September 22, 1881.
[15] Johnson, Emeroy, A Church Planted.
[16] Minutes, Minnesota Conference, 1869. Mimeographed copy. "Once each before the next Conference meeting."
[17] Johnson, Emeroy, A Church Planted, p. 287-293.
[18] Langford, Norman F., Fire Upon the Earth, p. 187. Westminster Press. By permission.
[19] Skaffaren, September 10, 1890, p. 6. "Diary of J. Magney, from Trip in Morrison, Stearns and Todd Counties."
[20] Minutes, Augustana Synod, 1873, p. 27.
[21] Ibid, 1895, p. 17.
[22] Ibid, 1876, p. 27.
[23] Ibid, 1874, p. 8, 9.

III. DEVELOPMENT

Pressing North

"Who is there that does not know one thing or another about this eulogized (Red River) Valley? Barrels of printers ink and tons of paper, not to mention all golden-tongued orators, have tried to make its fame as great as the sea."[1] It took some time before the Swedes ventured out of the woods unto the prairies of the Red River Valley. It has been suggested that because the chinchbugs devastated the crops in the eastern sections of Minnesota, the people were compelled to find new land. In the year 1811 a Scotchman, Thomas Douglas, together with others settled in the neighborhood of Pembina. Later he moved northward. In 1840 the Hudson Bay Company established a trading post and built a revenue office there, also a post office. In 1862 the steamer "International" came up the Red River as far as Moorhead. The same year the Indian uprising took place. In 1870 United States soldiers came into this territory and eight years later the St. Paul, Minneapolis, and Manitoba railroad had been completed as far as St. Vincent. A Swedish captain, Enstrom, was the first auditor in Kittson county. Mr. and Mrs. Erick Norland came in the year 1870. Mrs. Norland was the first Swedish woman in the county.[2]

In 1881 Dr. Sjoblom, as President of the Conference, reported: "Besides the 123 congregations of which 46 are vacant, and our great mission fields in southwest Minnesota and Dakota, northwest and northern Minnesota, we have now received the Red River Valley which is being settled with surprising rapidity. I am told that about six hundred immigrants pass through St. Paul every day headed for the valley and a large portion are Swedes. Many come directly from Sweden and some move westward from eastern sections of our country." [3] We have already given reason for the immigration northwestward, but there were several other contributing factors. Thus Jonas Swenson reports to the Synod in 1873: "With a few exceptions there has been an increase in membership in the congregations and new congregations have been organized. The exceptions in this situation call our attention to the difficulties under which we labor in this country, more than any other—the constant moving of the people from one place to another. The congregations are weakened and many of the roving countrymen become scattered and are finally lost to the church." Other obstacles and problems appear, as we read: "In many places dissensions have been caused by spiritual adventurers from Sweden, who pretended to be preachers of the Gospel, but soon were discovered to be deceivers and partisans, some even being guilty before civil law." [4]

Typical of the pioneer period is the account of Nels Malm who in 1879 made a business trip to Crookston. There he met a Peter Jarvis who convinced him that the "cream of the valley" was the country around Louisa (Argyle) and induced him to make a trip north from Crookston to see about prospects for settlements. Between Crookston and Louisa he passed only two buildings—one of these in Warren. It was in March and most of the snow had melted on the prairies. He came up on the railroad which had just been completed.

Mr. Malm was so impressed with the land that upon returning to Willmar he organized a party for the North. They left Willmar in eight covered wagons travelling overland to Argyle. Mr. Malm and one other among the men walked, driving a herd of sixty-two cows. It took them twenty-four days and they arrived in Argyle November 4, 1879.

On December 15, 1879, Mr. Charles A. Berglund, agent for the Cunard Steamship Line, coming directly from Sweden, made a call at Warren and was so well impressed that he expected to send one hundred families to settle there. [5]

29

Pastor J. O. Cavallin, then pastor in Moorhead, made visits to the northern sections of the Valley. His first "safari" was in April, 1881. One of the members of his church, Mr. Sundberg, urged him to make the trip. Because it rained continuously for two days the roads were impassable. While he was waiting at a hotel in Hallock an old man came in, and when he saw Pastor Cavallin, he exclaimed: "O God, shall I once more see one of our pastors." In May of the same year a second pastoral visit was made by Cavallin. "I preached," he relates, "at the Lars Eklund and J. P. Strandberg homes to ten or twelve people and conducted a holy communion service when Mr. Sundberg was the only one who communed. This was the first communion service in Kittson county.[6] There were no baptisms." "My next visit through the valley was June 13 and 14 when also the settlements further south were visited. One always got good impressions of the people during the pioneer period, though poverty and privations were grinning horribly in many places. I always considered the whole Red River Valley as a new Skåne."[7] Cavallin was the first pastor in this particular territory. Pastor Jonas G. Lagerstrom of St. Peter, Minnesota, labored here one month, being sent by the Conference. At a meeting held during the middle of September at the Lars Eklund home it was decided to organize a congregation.

> "Notice is hereby given that a meeting will be held for the organization of a Swedish Evangelical Lutheran church and for selection of officers for said church, at the residence of Lars Mattson in section 24, town of Red River, at 10:00 A.M. October 8, 1881."[8]

Pastor L. P. Lundquist visited Warren and Red River in 1882. He reports in part: "I preached twice, the first time in the Mortenson home, the second time in a school house. One Sunday afternoon I preached in Kennedy—in a store building under construction. Generally I led the singing myself, but at the communion service in the school house in Red River there was one man who tried to lead the singing and sang the Psalm 154 to all the melodies in the Psalmbook." [9]

"In Labors Abundant"

It was not only the pioneer homesteaders and early settlers who endured the hardships, but the trailblazing pastors shared the trials. Pastor L. A. Hocanzon has given a very graphic account of his experiences as a home missionary. He writes under the title: "Memories from the Mission Field, 1883."

"I was called by the mission board of the Minnesota Conference to work on the mission field in the Red River Valley for a period of six months, during 1883. On April 22—my birthday—I started. I had a few addresses of people living in the vicinity of Warren. The first stop was to be at Kennedy. I had written a Mr. Mortenson to meet me and also to announce services for the next day. There was no one to meet me, but Mr. Mortenson had arranged for the services to be held at his house. Kennedy had only a hotel and a store. A land company owned 40,000 acres around there. There was a farmer at the station, who offered to take me with him and he would bring me to the Mortenson home the next day. The roads were exceptionally bad. The snow was two feet deep, but soft and wet. We could only drive at a slow gait. It was impossible to follow the tracks and the sleigh sank deep into the snow.

"The next day it rained very heavily, but nevertheless he brought his family along to the services. This time he used a wagon. It was a long distance and traveling was difficult. Approaching the Mortenson home we drove into a ditch which we had not noticed because of the snow. With difficulty we unhitched the horses and with some help by the church people we also got the vehicle out. All the time it kept on raining. We were all able to walk to the house, except 'grandma' who sat in the cold and rain for two hours. Even though she wore a fur coat she was drenching wet.

31

"I became acquainted with the people present and found them very friendly. Many had come from Goodhue county and some from Scandian Grove in Nicollet county and were church trained. During the summer I made many visits to a congregation named Red River.

"In the Warren congregation Peter Dahlquist lived out in the country. He was of much assistance to me in the congregation—in fact he meant a great deal to the work of the church in the entire valley. I held a number of services here, one at the Dahlquist home and one in town. The school house was for sale and I bought it for the congregation at a very reasonable price. It had a very favorable location and was used for church purposes for a considerable period of time.

"East of Stephen was a Swedish colony of people who recently had come from the northern part of Sweden. Many had been in Ström, Jämtland and had attended the school of Michael Sandell. I organized a congregation here and made repeated visits here. The name of the church was Salem. It was later joined with Warren as a parish. East of Hallock was another new colony. Here a congregation was organized adopting the name Saron.

"Eighteen miles east of Argyle lived a few Swedes, among them a man whose wife kept house for me after the death of my first wife. He invited me to his home. He had done some preaching. Since it was threshing time we were unable to hire any kind of conveyance. Having walked thirteen miles I borrowed a bony horse from a Norwegian farmer. But to sit on the bare back, with only a sack, was very uncomfortable. When we arrived at the house—which was so small that the man had carried home the lumber for it on his back—it began to rain and continued for three days. Nevertheless, we had services, confirmation and communion. In spite of the rain the house was filled and many were satisfied to stand outside, as long as they could be along. On the third day I continued the journey early—going horseback. When I borrowed the horse Hans Egen had promised to take me home when I came

Dr. S. W. Swenson
President R. R. V. Conference
1912-1922

Aug. Lundgren
Treasurer R. R. V. Conference
1912-1932

Emil E. Gahlon
Treasurer R. R. V. Conference
1932-

Pastor J. Edor Larson
Author of History of R. R. V.
Conference

back; but now he refused. 'If I take out my horses in this rain,' he said, 'I will ruin them for the rest of the year.' I had no recourse, but to walk, though I had quite a heavy baggage. The grass was tall and the black, sticky clay was soft mire. Soon my shoes were filled with muddy water and my feet began to swell. I tried several times along the way to hire a rig, but in vain. All gave the same excuse as the Norwegian. There was nothing to do, but to trudge onward.

"When I came within three miles of the railroad station I could not follow the road any further, as it was deep and filled with water. Along the sides was a plowed field, very uneven and rough. When I was half a mile from the station my strength gave way. It got dark before my eyes and there was nothing I could do, but to sigh to God. Having stood still a while, my strength returned and I came finally to a restaurant where one of my confirmands worked. A man pulled off my boots and emptied the muddy water on the clean floor. The proprietress came with a broom threatening to chase us out; but by giving her an extra tip I was permitted to stay and order dinner. For a long time I could wear nothing on my feet but rubbers. I caught the train at 12:30 p.m. and went on my way to Winnipeg, wet as I was.

"In October 1883 I made my last trip through the 'Valley' to arrange for the calling of pastors. I had preached in Beckville in the forenoon and at night I took the train for Warren. The train was late, so it was three o'clock in the afternoon when I arrived. Mr. P. Dahlquist was there to meet me as always. He had his mule team along and gave me the best one to ride; but it performed so many acrobatic stunts that we arrived at the school house late. We had communion service, conducted a business meeting and called a pastor. Immediately after the meeting we left for Warren where the schedule was the same. It was time to hurry to the station to take the train for Stephen. Mr. Dahlquist went along as delegate from Salem. We arrived there after midnight. A blizzard was raging all night and the snowfall was heavy. We rested a while on the dirt floor in a shanty, which a man who worked on the coal dock had built for himself. He was a member of the church and his family lived in the country.

"I had a promise to get horses for the trip to the church, but because of the storm we could get none. We were compelled to walk eleven miles in deep snow and tall grass. The gophers had dug up the fields so that the ground was very uneven. It was to take one step high and the next low. We arrived at eleven o'clock. First we had communion service, then a business meeting. A man from the shanty where we slept was with us. He had been there the previous Sunday and warned the people not to join in parish fellowship with Warren, because they would then never get to have their own pastor. He thought the same rules pertained here as in Sweden. I talked to the people for two hours before I could prevail upon them to call a pastor.

"It was already dusk when we were through. We had nothing to eat that day, except a very meager breakfast. I asked for some food and got a glass of milk and a piece of bread, but nothing was offered to Dahlquist. After considerable dickering we finally got a man to take us on our way. It was a slow ride and we had to detour because of the work of the gophers. This made the distance sixteen miles to Stephen. Late at night we arrived at the hospitable Lundeen home. Dead tired, frozen through and dreadfully hungry we were—but the pastor who was called accepted the call.

"In a similar way, but without special difficulties, communion services and elections were held in the other congregations. Many of the members had received religious training under Norelius and others.

"I made three trips to Winnipeg. I was told there were many Swedes. Arriving I had neither names nor addresses. I searched a whole day before I found a Swede. He was a

34

water hauler by the name of Petterson and had joined the Methodist church. He introduced me to his pastor who gave me permission to have our services in his church. He was a genuine Christian who bewailed the fact that there were five Methodist churches in Winnipeg—all different. He suffered real persecution. The church was filled with Swedes at the evening service. I also did some calling. Where we now have the most valuable business district of the city there were then only tarpaper shacks—and there were hundreds of them. I baptized a number of children. The men were away at work and the women were at home with the children. One of the Swedes had a boarding house which was simply a board shanty with partitions along the sides as in cattle barns. In each 'stall' was room for eight men to sleep, four in the lower and four in the upper 'berths.' All the stalls were filled with men playing cards, while the whisky bottles were standing in the windows. It looked hideous.

"The second trip was a continuation of the before-mentioned visit to Argyle. When I arrived late in the evening, it had rained for three days and the streets were so thoroughly soaked, that the streetcars were stalled when the rails and ties sank in the mire. The streetcars even froze solid in the mud and the streets were smooth as glass. I had a good distance to walk before I came to a home where I had been promised quarters. They had no fuel and I slept—soaked as I was—in a cold room. Sunday I had services with about seventy-five taking communion. I baptized one child and made several calls.

"My third visit was in connection with the previously mentioned business meetings. It was winter and cold. Sunday it was forty below and windy. I was invited to stay at a hotel because a young lady there was to be married and I was asked to perform the ceremony. They served a big dinner. I had some difficulty to find out how I could legally perform the marriage. I asked a lawyer, but he did not know, yet he charged me two dollars for his 'services.' The old Methodist pastor finally enlightened me." [10]

The president of the Conference comments as follows: "The report of Pastor Hocanzon presents the story of the missionary efforts in the Red River Valley, where he visited Warren, Argyle and Stephen in Marshall county, Kennedy and Hallock in Kittson county and Winnipeg. His work has consisted in preaching, performing baptisms, confirming, conducting communion services, making pastoral calls, spiritual counselling, preparing for the confirmation classes and Sunday schools, organizing congregations and arranging and conducting business meetings." [11]

Rightly is this work evaluated in the "Century of Life and Growth": "The indefatigable missionary, L. A. Hocanzon, came into the Red River Valley. This vast valley in northern Minnesota had begun to fill up with settlers, attracted by its good wheat farming opportunities." [12] Looking back once more we read at the time of his pastoral services: "At last the Red River Valley has received a shepherd, but his time and strength is not sufficient for the many tasks there. We are thinking of calling two more pastors, but even so we will only be supplied in the regular congregations." [13]

In his second annual report Dr. S. W. Swenson, President of the Red River Valley Conference, refers to the early settlers: "The people who dared to venture into these regions between the years 1875 and 1879 were considered foolhardy adventurers who did not value their lives very highly. . . . We owe a great debt of gratitude to these noble pioneers. Here as elsewhere in the Synod, the work of the church was carried on amidst prayer, sacrifices and hope." [14]

They Are Still Coming

Immigrants from far-off Sweden continued to arrive, their faces ever turned north and westward.

"On March 11, 1888, Lars, Ellis and I, together with Mr. and Mrs. Nels Lundquist and two children, Mr. and Mrs. Erick Sjoberg and six children, Mr. A. Markstrom and daughter, Peter Fredricks and John Sandberge left our dear ones in Wilhelmina, Sweden, for the wonderful land of America. For eighteen days and eighteen hours we were on the ocean. The going was rough, so that practically everyone was seasick. The Lundquists met us in Nelson Park, Minnesota, about ten miles east of Stephen. They had arrived two weeks before us and thought that we had perished since we were so late in arriving.

"Wickstrom, Lundquist, Sjoberg and a Mr. Eric Holm all went on ahead to see what the land was like near Roseau. Mr. Holm had a yoke of oxen so he acted as guide. In June we ladies left for Roseau. The trip took four days. Our little son, Ellis, was very sick so I held him almost all the way. The third night we came to Badger Creek which was at flood stage. The men made a makeshift bridge of poplar trees. On the other side a man offered to carry my baby, but since he was a stranger I refused at first. Finally I consented and he took me to a tent where there were two women. They laid Ellis on a cot and gave me some water to give him. As he could not swallow I soaked a cloth and put on his lips. This did not help very much and he died in a few minutes. I stayed there over night and can truthfully say that it was the longest night of my life.

"In the morning Eric Holm came to get us. After a terrible ride over rough roads we finally reached the place where my husband was. This was on the bank of the river, about five miles from the site of Roseau. . . . We decided to go to the farm so Lars went to get the boat which was loaned us. I rowed the boat while Lars took the wagon and the cattle across. Crossing the prairies the mosquitoes were so bad we could hardly breathe. We finally came to the home of an Irish family. They had a dog which frightened our oxen so

37

they ran back to the river, getting us all wet. We all had to get out as best we could. Lars had to swim backwards to get the cattle and our belongings from the river. Mr. Sutton, the storekeeper, watched in amazement as we worked to salvage our belongings. We motioned to him that we could not speak English. He provided us with a tent in which we spent the night. In the morning he came with a pound of '4x' coffee. But I had nothing to cook it in and as he could not understand what I wanted I found an empty syrup can in which I cooked it. I crushed the coffee beans with an empty bottle on a paper sack. In that way we had our first coffee here.

"In December 1890 the little log church was finished so we could have our services in it for the first time.

"We also thought we should have a Ladies Aid, so when Pastor Askelund was here we got together a small group. We were only four until the latter part of the summer. The very first items we worked for was a washbasin, pail, dipper and a piece of material to drape off a corner as a washroom for the pastor. We made money by carding, spinning, knitting socks and mittens, selling or trading them to the storekeeper for what we needed. Though these days were not too pleasant, yet it was a time we shall not forget." [15]

Pastor Gustaf Peterson describes a preaching trip in 1885. "I never knew a time when I was so close to death as then. When we came to the place I could only talk with greatest difficulty; I was so frozen that it took a good while before I was thawed out enough so the services could begin." [16]

We have followed the immigrants marching northward along the Red River Valley, and now we must go back and take up the course of events in and about the center of the territory we have described.

New Frontiers

The region which is now Moorhead was being settled in 1871. The first locomotive reached the city just before Christmas that year. Immigration was rapid from Europe, especially from the Scandinavian countries and the railroad companies were anxious to bring the people west. According to reports to the Conference three pastors had been called to do mission work in the Red River Valley—P. Nordgren, S. J. Kronberg and L. Johnson—but none of them could accept. It was therefore resolved that the Alexandria District be asked to visit Moorhead and Fargo with the preaching of the Word of God, in connection with its May meeting and that half of the travelling expenses be paid out of the mission treasury. Pastor Cavallin writes: "In March 1878 I visited these regions on invitation from a pious man who had moved to Cass county, North Dakota, from southern Minnesota. I preached in the 'Erickson House' — hotel — Moorhead. There were ten or twelve in the dining room, while in the next room they were worshiping Bacchus—the god of alcohol. To the credit of Mr. Erickson it should be mentioned, that he cautioned the topers to be quiet because a Swedish preacher was conducting a service in the next room. After the services he came and thanked me for the visit, though he never heard a word of the sermon. I did not surmise then that two years afterwards a congregation was to be organized there and I was to be their pastor. Though it seemed spiritually parched and dead, God had some who cried for the Bread of Life." [17]

A congregation was organized in Moorhead May 4, 1880. Fourteen persons applied as charter members, but only eleven —four couples and three single men—were active members. There was considerable opposition to the church. A Swedish woman warned all against the Lutheran church and also said that she prayed that God would spare Moorhead from an Augustana pastor. The editor of the newspaper of the city wrote an abusive article against the church, saying that the pastor would soon be run out of town if he did not stop disturbing the peace by his preaching of repentance. Two years later the editor apologized through his father. You cannot stop the avalanche which slowly moves down the valley, nor can the Kingdom of God be stopped where God has given open doors. The first church building in Moorhead consisted of a school house which the congregation bought for $2,500 and remodelled for church and parsonage. The upper story was the church auditorium "where kerosene lamps provided light and a big oblong woodburning stove made the winter's chill bearable." [18]

Westward We Go

The tent stakes were moved and the horizons were widened as the immigrants, like a spring flood, moved into new territory. From Minnesota the settlers headed west into the vast prairies of the Dakotas, and we are here concerned with North Dakota. Jonas Auslund, president of the Conference, reports to the Synod in 1877: "Pastor L. A. Hocanzon and Pastor H. P. Quist have worked in the fields along the St. Paul and Sioux City Railroad and made trips into the North Dakota territory, where many of our countrymen have sought homes for themselves. Heartrending cries for help have reached our ears, that they may have a pastor stationed in their midst, that more may be done for them than an occasional visit. We can apply to the churches in North Dakota the words of the prophet: 'O thou afflicted, tossed with tempests and not comforted' (Is. 54:11). All kinds of sects have made great efforts to scatter these congregations and draw the members to themselves. But the Lord has looked to his distressed flock and kept it from the wolf." [19] Pastor Andrew Jackson, president of the Minnesota Conference, reports in 1880: "Our large mission fields, besides the many vacant congregations, cause us continually work and worry. Besides Minnesota we now have as our field North Dakota where many of our countrymen have moved." [20]

From the report to the Conference meeting at Marine Mills, Minnesota, October 11-17, 1881, we quote:

"Because of the report from Pastor Cavallin and a communication from the Church Council at Moorhead, resolved·

1. That the Conference supports the congregation in Moorhead with $300 on condition that Pastor Cavallin be permitted to make three or four extensive missionary trips through Dakota.

2. That work be begun in Fargo, but that the people there are considered to be in position to pay the rental for a hall."

Pastor Cavallin is in a way the father of the church work in North Dakota. Well may we cite here the later words of a Historian of the Minnesota Conference: "With sincere enthusiasm and an unflinching faithfulness to the countrymen in dispersion he has carried on an important mission work in North Dakota for many years." [21] From Moorhead this missionary extended his interests and travels to the capital of the State. We heard Pastor Cavallin say that he remembered the city of Bismarck when it had only a few board sidewalks, which were even dangerous to use because they were so poorly nailed. But this did not deter the missionary from walking the streets of the city in quest for souls. He was working for the Master. As a result of his missionary efforts a congregation was organized in Bismarck in January, 1883. [22]

Since the anchor posts for the temple of the church of Christ had been established in the eastern and western parts of the State, the next task was to expand the work in all directions. The distances were great and the settlements were small, but the Gospel was brought to the groups. Pastor S. Udden was missionary in Barnes and Steele counties. He reported in 1889 that there were three congregations organized— Bismarck; Bethany, Burleigh county and Hofva, Steele county. Pastor A. Melin, J. A. Johnson, S. J. Kronberg and L. Johnson made extensive missionary journeys in the territory in 1891. Pastor Spångberg was missionary in Bismarck and Slaughter 1890-1895 and was followed by Pastor L. E. Gullander. As the population increased congregations were organized. Thus we find White Stone Hills, 1889; Nebo, Valley City, 1890; Elim, Fargo, 1891. A correspondent (J.P.N.M.) writes from Rutland, N. D., in 1894: "In this region we have a considerable number of our countrymen and especially here in Rutland where only a few Americans live. The industry and perseverance of our people have come into evidence. There is no church in Oakes, but quite a number of Swedes. Ten Lutheran families live in and around the town." [23] A congregation was organized at Oakes, August 26, 1905. "In the latter part of October (1894) five pastors from the Alexandria District made a trip to Sargent and Dickey counties, North Dakota, in order to encourage and edify the countrymen by means of the preached Word." [24]

In 1909 the Executive Committee of the Minnesota Conference reported that "at the first of the year Pastor J. O. Cavallin was called as a traveling missionary in North Dakota for a period of six months," but later the same year it is stated [25] that "he has now a permanent call for this position." He was not only a zealous home missionary, but also a good reporter in the church press and at Conference meetings. In his words the Minnesota Conference "has a mission field larger than many a nation. Wherever we go in cities, villages or in the rural areas we find countrymen who are drifting away." [26] There were encouragements for the servant of the Lord: "The many and long journeys have often been very tiresome, but the receptiveness of the people has caused one to forget all this." The church at large was mindful of the "excellent work" performed by the "missionary to whom God gave health and special interest in this effort of gathering our scattered people and organizing them into congregations." [27]

There was an element of determination and perseverance

in the efforts of these pioneering pastors. "I dare say, that there is an open door. . . . Because of experiences as a home missionary in the Red River Valley and North Dakota, it is my firm conviction, that one of the conditions for success and victory is not to surrender a field, where work has been started, even in the face of difficulties, nor merely experiment in church activity. . . . Where we find enough people to organize a little congregation, this ought to be done, but merely to organize a congregation and afterwards leave it to its own fate, is utter irresponsibility." [28] Not only was the missionary well received, but the entire District "deserves a special mention because of the missionary zeal it has shown and the work which has been accomplished. The support of the Conference has been well used." Even in the face of such trial as crop failures the laborers did not lose courage, but threw themselves into the work "body and soul." There was not only sowing, but also reaping. "From a few sections it is reported that the breezes of the Spirit of God have been in evidence so that fields which have long been fallow have revived and our work is doubly successful. We rejoice over this fact. New fields have been opened and we rejoice in additional workers."

Well does the writer remember how happy the veteran missionary, Cavallin, was when he was remembered on his birthday. We shall let him tell it in his own words. "With gratefulness I will continue my humble efforts as health and strength permit, until God and the Conference retire me. Finally, I perhaps ought to mention that the day I was seventy came the brethren, N. P. Tuleen, J. Edor Larson and J. E. Liljedahl, to our home and brought congratulatory greetings and a love gift of $240 from our people in North Dakota." [29]

Into the Woods the Master Went

Turning once more to the original starting point, the Alexandria District, we want to follow the beginnings in what is now the Bemidji District. The Gospel "invasion" came from two directions. First from the west and northwest as we see from a roll call of "birthdays" of congregations—St. John, Fertile, 1881; Salem, McIntosh and Lima, Erskine, 1886; Poplar Lake, Fosston, 1887; Asphult, Fosston, 1889. From the south came missionaries to Bemidji and vicinity. The pastors of the Alexandria District extended their interests towards the north. The missionary who especially centered his activities in this section was Pastor J. H. Randahl, who visited the small groups of countrymen scattered in the deep woods. A number of the places where he called and where he worked are no longer on the map of our Church, yet his labors even there were not in vain. He brought the Manna of Life to the people in the "wilderness." [30]

We want to call to the special attention one of the congregations in this District, because it is the result of a somewhat planned colonization. The Augustana Colonization Company of Minneapolis, headed by Pastor C. E. Elving, selected a little flag station on the Great Northern Railroad, about twenty-five miles north of Bemidji, as a suitable spot for planned settlement. People from Illinois, Minnesota, and North Dakota came and bought land. Urban people turned tillers of the soil where clearing the land was a gigantic task. But the little village, which consisted of a hotel, store, post office, one house and a number of tarpaper shacks was within a few years transformed into a neat little community where in 1940 "all except one family belonged to church." The first Lutheran service in Hines was held in the consolidated school house Sunday, July 25, 1915, conducted by Pastor J. H. Randahl. November 10, 1915, a congregation was organized. The congregation bought five acres of land with timber on root. The members cut the logs, two men sawed and planed the lumber at their mill. The erection of the church and parsonage was a co-operative project by all the members. The land was cleared of stumps and became the cemetery. The writer conducted the first committal in the new God's acre. A young girl was buried. Only a small

44

patch was cleared at the time, but it was a very impressive service. A sheaf, a first fruit, was gathered into the heavenly garner.

In Retrospect

As these early congregations were organized it became evident that in every community were hungering souls, Christians who were the spiritual children of revivals in Sweden. Others became conscious of the fact that man does not live by bread alone—especially when the bread is scanty and the people are few.

In many instances there were, as we have noted, revivals which brought spiritual life to many. The Civil War, like all wars, had an unwholesome influence upon the people. During the postwar era a restless, speculative spirit of worldliness prevailed and the former simplicity had disappeared. Then came the reconstruction period with its trials. The former self-confidence and self-sufficiency gave way to the enlightenment of the Word of God.[31]

As we have noted, there was a concern for home mission which may be expressed in the modern term of Parish Evangelism. Our people met the great challenge of the day. They were not so conscious of methods as of the responsibility of each Christian for his fellow men. And yet there were times when they thought of methods. An article in Minnesota *Stats Tidning,* January 25, 1905, over the signature of Dr. J. A. Krantz suggests a setup very much like the one now used in the Augustana Church. "We believe it would greatly enhance our missionary work, if in each of the larger mission Districts, where many of our countrymen live or move, we had missionary superintendents who were not bound by parish call, but could supervise the entire field, arrange the work and prepare for the organization of congregations and the formation of parishes. He would know and see where the greatest efforts should be put forth and himself have a hand in it, or call upon someone else to help him. Together with the Mission Board he would be empowered to call suitable pastors and to move them." [32]

References

[1] Skaffaren, May 2, 1890, p. 4. "W" in "Omnibus."
[2] Lundgren, L. P., Minne i ord och bild. p. 11, 9.
[3] Minutes, Augustana Synod, 1881, p. 23.
[4] Ibid, 1873, p. 7, 10.
[5] Warren Sheaf, July 4, 1952.
[6] Korsbaneret, 1906, p. 108.
[7] Lundgren, L. P., Minne i ord och bild, "Skane"—southern province of Sweden, particularly fertile.
[8] Ibid, p. 22.
[9] Ibid, p. 54.
[10] Korsbaneret, 1915, pp. 103-111.
[11] Minutes, Minnesota Conference, 1884, p. 16.
[12] Century of Life and Growth, p. 54.
[13] Minutes, Minnesota Conference, 1884, p. 16.
[14] Minutes, R.R.V. Conference, 1913, p. 13.
[15] Mrs. Lars Wickstrom in Letter to the Church at Roseau, Minnesota, on its Fiftieth Anniversary, 1940. Written from Chariton, Iowa. Anniversary Book, p. 45.
[16] Lundgren, L. P. Minne i ord och b.ld, p. 61.
[17] Korsbaneret, 1906, p. 108.
  Pastor Magney extended his journey in (August) 1871 into this region. He reports: "My trip north went well and after a month I returned safe and sound. From Buffalo river I travelled northwest through Clay county to the Red River, which I reached at the little town of Georgetown (fifteen miles north of Fargo). The land along the Red River is level like a calm sea. It is unoccupied except for a narrow strip along the river. I spent about two weeks time on the Dakota side of the river between Georgetown and Abercrombie, a distance of fifty miles. I preached four times in three places, baptized several children and performed one marriage. Continued then on to Fergus Falls, where I stayed three and a half days and preached each evening. In time this will undoubtedly become a sizeable city. If I get a chance to visit this place again this fall I plan to organize a congregation." Missionaren, January 1872, p. 5-6.
[18] Anderson, Mrs. Chas. L. History of the Bethesda Church, Moorhead, Minnesota. In Manuscript.
[19] Minutes, Augustana Synod, 1877, p. 20.
  Minutes of the Minnesota Conference meeting, October 7, 1878, contain the following: "A Committee reported: In order to investigate what steps should be taken to establish a mission in Fargo, Moorhead and surrounding regions, Pastor A. P. Monten was sent."
  "Because of this report, resolved that the Executive Committee be instructed: 1. To call a home missionary for an indefinite period and that he has his headquarters in Fargo and work there as well as in the neighboring territory."
  Minutes, Minnesota Conference, 1879, p. 4. (First printed Minutes.)
[20] Ibid, 1880, p. 20.
  "In North Dakota is not a single Augustana pastor in active service." (Augustana, March 19, 1896.)
[21] Lund, Emil. Minnesota konferensens historia, Vol. I, p. 87.
[22] Olson, Miss Mabel. Historical Sketch of First Lutheran Church, Bismarck. In Manuscript.
[23] Skaffaren, June 20, 1894.
[24] Ibid, December 5, 1894.
[25] Minutes, Minnesota Conference, 1909, p. 57.
[26] Ibid, 1910, p. 50.
[27] Ibid, 1910, p. 28.
[28] Ibid, 1912, p. 27.

[29] Ibid, 1914, p. 50.
[30] Minnesota Stats Tidning, February 22, 1911.
[31] Evangelisk Tidskrift, 1878, p. 54.
"Then came the great awakening," writes S. J. Kronberg in "Banbrytar-en." "A loving God began to awaken the unbelievers and I noticed that those who had communed often and received the body and the blood of Christ unworthily were among the first to realize their condition. Where there is hunger for the Word of God no obstacles are permitted to interfere. People traveled eighteen miles on foot to attend services and returned home the same day. Prayer week was extended to two weeks with meetings twice a day. Those who came to the church first were singing, praying and meditating until the pastor came." p. 220.
[32] Minnesota Stats Tidning, January 25, 1905.

IV. ORGANIZATION

The Formation of the Red River Valley Conference

In the Minutes of the Alexandria District, December 12, 1896, we find the following: "Referring to the circular communication from the Red River Valley District regarding the division of the Conference, Resolved,

> that the Alexandria District does not consider the time ripe for such a division, but is of the opinion that the Conference should contribute more from its missionary funds to this section of the Conference in order that greater missionary efforts might be put forth on the tremendously large fields in Northwestern Minnesota."

We hear nothing more said about this matter until 1902 when Pastor James Moody suggests in a newspaper item that the Minnesota Conference be divided. The underlying reason seems to have been the fact that supporters of Northwestern College felt that their efforts in behalf of this school were ignored or opposed by those who favored Gustavus Adolphus College. The suggestion naturally created a lively discussion in the church and secular press. The arguments were many and varied. The whole question at times was dismissed with the curt statement that "to divide the Conference is a thought that is too absurd for thinking men." [1] Others stressed the fact that the Minnesota Conference was smaller than the Kansas Conference. Further, with "the exception of the southern half, the entire Conference (Minnesota) is a great mission field. Would it then be feasible to divide it, in order to carry on more efficient work?" "Very little of the mission money is spent where it is gathered." In answer to this comes the statement, that "the northwestern part is isolated from the rest and has its own special interests. The missionary efforts in behalf of this section have been very lame." [2] The arguments—pro and con—continue. In regard to the missionary work—the northwest has twenty-five self-supporting pastorates, has many mission fields, is receiving streams of settlers from North Dakota and Sweden. Yet this section of the Conference has not much to say about the work as such, since it has never even had a member in the Executive Committee.

The president of the Minnesota Conference, Dr. J. A. Krantz, discussed the question of division in his annual message. He said:

"In connection with the mission work and its prosecution I want to bring to the serious consideration of the Conference if the time is not ripe for a sane and natural division. The more attention I have given to the fields and their needs as well as the opportunities which beckon us on every side, the more I have become convinced of the impossibility of carrying on this work successfully as we now are organized. If we had many more workers at our disposal it might be possible, but as it is, we must see one field after another slip out of our hands or see how the work for a long time to come will be retarded and be made more difficult because we come only after the fields have been scorched by the activities of the sects, or when we have lost the people we so badly needed in building our church. I believe the only sensible division at present should be according to State lines. North and South Dakota should each constitute a Conference and if they during the year received help in the arrangement of the respective fields and thus also received a few more workers, they could easily take care of their mission interests. I think such a step would call forth resources and gifts which hitherto have not been surmised. Immigration by our people is on the increase year by year, which should make the work of the New Conferences very hopeful." [3]

The Resolutions on the president's report contain the following:

"Whereas two Districts have petitioned for the division of the Conference and because of the extensive territory and the resulting difficulties in the prosecution of the many-complexioned work, and for other reasons, the Conference considers it paramount that the question of division be decided now, thus preventing an agitation and an uncertainty of mind which eventually would hinder the work of the Conference,

Therefore resolved, that a committee consisting of one pastor and one layman from each District and a representative from each of the Conference Institutions, with the president of the Conference as chairman, be elected; and that this committee submit at the next Conference meeting a plan as to the number and boundaries of the new Conferences; taking into account the mission fields, the schools and other institutions; and that this report be published in the Augustana and Minnesota *Stats Tidning* at least two weeks prior to the next Conference meeting." [4]

The committee, which consisted of twenty-three pastors and sixteen laymen, reported, advising that the Minnesota Conference be divided into "three Conferences with distinct boundaries and that Canada be a Conference of its own."

After an intense and thorough discussion an informal ballot was taken which resulted in 152 votes in favor of division and 146 against. During the lively discussion that followed it was brought out very definitely, that in the general opinion of the delegation the Conference covers too much territory and that a division is desirable, but not "according to the radical way the committee suggested, but so that State lines, as far as possible, be boundaries."

Finally the following resolution was adopted by a large majority: "That the Conference remains intact, but it encourages the congregations distant from the center to try to unite in forming a new Conference." [5]

The little flame which had been kindled was smouldering, but it was kept aglow. The minutes of the Alexandria District, May 16-19, 1910, contain this item: "Resolved, that the invitation from the Fargo District to the officers of the Alexandria District, to meet with them next July for a discussion of the question of the formation of a new Conference, be accepted." [6] The Districts along the western edge of the State of Minnesota presented a petition for permission to organize. Dr. J. A. Krantz reports in his message:

"Petition for the formation of a new Conference in the northwestern part of the State is submitted for action. This matter has since our last meeting taken a new turn. The North Dakota District has decided to remain in the Minnesota Conference. The only person in the Big Stone District who was personally interested in the matter, has moved to another Conference and the District will not secede. Within the Alexandria District the opinions differ as yet, and all are not united in the matter within the Red River District. If a new Conference were to be formed now, it would consist of a small section which would seem very unnatural. It is advisable that this question be postponed until this region has had a chance to develop so that a natural division can take place. For this section to constitute a separate Conference were only to cut it off from the sources of support and help it would need in the undeveloped sections of the State." [7]

Representatives from the Alexandria, Red River, and North Dakota Districts met in Stillwater, Minnesota, February 24, 1911, at which meeting a resolution was adopted petitioning the Minnesota Conference, that the named three Districts be permitted to form a new Conference.[8] In so doing they referred to the statements in the president's message the previous year.[9]

The Minnesota *Stats Tidning,* March 22, 1911, carried the following:

Announcement

"Hereby all pastors in the Big Stone District, who desire to join in the organization of a new Conference in the northwest, and all pastors in the Fargo, Red River, and North Dakota Districts of the Minnesota Conference of the Evangelical Lutheran Augustana Synod are called to meet in the Swedish Lutheran Church, Moorhead, Minnesota, Tuesday, April 4, 1911. The meeting begins April 4, at 8:00 P.M., with divine services and communion.

"The pastors should see that each congregation is represented by a lay delegate who may, in behalf of his congregation, speak and vote pro or con in the matter of forming a new Conference. This is not to be understood as a rebellion against the Minnesota Conference, because at the meeting of that body in St. Peter, 1910, the following resolution was adopted: 'That the congregations further removed from the center of the Conference be encouraged to organize themselves into a new Conference and present to the (Minnesota) Conference such a petition.' We must have this meeting in order to try to determine whether to organize a new Conference or have it as it is. By this means the uncertainty, which now paralyzes our work in the northwest, will be removed. Brethren of the clergy, come to this meeting. Congregations, see that you are represented at the meeting. If it seems good to us to remain status quo, then may we patiently and willingly bear the burdens placed upon us. If it does not seem wise as it is, then may we in the name of the Lord, try to organize a new Conference.

"That the Convention may be organized as quickly as possible I would ask each pastor and lay delegate to report to me in writing as soon as possible, if they intend to attend. Then I can have the roll call ready at the start of the meeting. "The Lord bless our Lutheran Church in the Northwest.

Lake Park, Minnesota, March 7, 1911.

Yours in Christ obliged,

N. Lehart."

Letters also were sent to the pastors and congregations of the Districts. The president of the Minnesota Conference called it all "deceiving and silly." He defended particularly his action in not presenting the Stillwater resolution, "because it came in late and had not been discussed" by the Executive Committee. And the report of the Conference committee—already referred to—"was not considered conducive to our church work and was therefore suppressed." [10]

Twenty-five pastors and fifty-one legally elected lay delegates, representing the three Districts and one pastor and one layman from the Big Stone District, met in Moorhead, Minnesota, and Fargo, North Dakota, April 4-5, 1911, to consider the question. Pro tempore officers elected were: Pastor N. Lehart, chairman; Pastor P. E. Ording, secretary. Later Pastor E. M. Erickson was elected chairman. The committee which had attended the Stillwater meeting, reported and presented seven theses for discussion, namely:

1. Can we better serve our church's interests in the northwest if we organize our own Conference?

2. Are we able to support a new Conference so that the work may not suffer?

3. Are we permitted by the constitution of the Synod and by the Minnesota Conference decisions to organize?

4. If we organize shall we present our petition directly to the Synod at its next convention or shall we first ask for the endorsement by the Conference?

5. If we organize our own Conference and make our ap-

plication to the Synod, what measures will we take to our own fields, that they may not lose the support?

6. What shall the attitude of the new Conference be toward the large indebtedness of the (Minnesota) Conference? Shall we assume responsibility for part of it?

7. If we organize how shall we look upon the debt which some congregations have accumulated by not paying in full their contributions to schools and missions? [11]

After a discussion of the above theses it was resolved that the first two questions be answered in the affirmative; that the assembly organize itself into a Conference and asks the Minnesota Conference for its recommendation to the Synod for sanction; that a committee be elected to prepare a constitution. At a later session held in the Elim church, Fargo, North Dakota, it was resolved that, the proposed constitution be distributed in the congregations; that a committee be elected to suggest a name; that the new Conference begins to function immediately after the next meeting of the Minnesota Conference; that the next meeting be held in Fergus Falls.

In his summary report from the Conference the president of the Synod reported: "At the annual meeting (of the Minnesota Conference) a petition was presented from pastors and congregations of the Alexandria, Fargo, and Red River Districts to organize a Conference, with the petition that the Minnesota Conference recommends to the Synod that this new Conference be organized and received." [12] "This petition was granted."

A petition from the newly organized Conference was presented to the Synod at its 1912 convention. A recommendation was also presented from the mother Conference:

To the Honorable President of the Augustana Synod, Dr. L. A. Johnston, Grace and Peace.
The Red River, Fargo, and Alexandria Districts at a joint

meeting at Moorhead, Minnesota, April 5, 1911, decided to petition the Conference for its endorsement to the Synod, that these Districts be permitted to organize themselves into a Conference.

By reason of this the Conference at its annual meeting in St. Peter, Minnesota, May 16-17, 1912, resolved:

1. That this petition be granted.

2. That the new Conference continues its obligations to the Minnesota Conference until the end of this conference year, February 1, 1913, regarding payments of budgets and financial obligations.

3. That the boundaries of the new Conference be as follows: To the east, the western edge of Betrami, Hubbard, Wadena and Todd counties; to the south the southern boundaries of Todd, Douglas, Grant and Wilkins counties, including Norunga in Pope county; to the west, the state line—though the congregations which now belong to the Red River and Fargo Districts shall belong to the new Conference; to the north, the Canadian boundary line.

Lafayette, Minnesota, May 25, 1913.
Respectfully,
S. A. Lindholm, Secretary of the Conference.

The Synod resolved:

1. That the petition of the newly formed Red River Valley Conference for admittance into the Synod be granted.

2. That its constitution be approved.

3. That the boundaries be determined in accordance with the decision of the Minnesota Conference.[13]

As already indicated the organization meeting was held in the Swedish Lutheran Church, Fergus Falls, Minnesota, May 24-27, 1912.

The resolutions relative to the petitioning to the Synod, as adopted at this meeting, have been quoted. Another resolution adopted at the same meeting is of importance.

"Inasmuch as the North Dakota District does not desire to belong to the new Conference, resolved:

That their petition in this matter to the Minnesota Conference be included in the minutes, in order that the historical development at the organization of the new Conference may be clarified to posterity. It reads:

1. That the North Dakota District gratefully recognizes that without the substantial aid of the Minnesota Conference, our District would not have been what it is to-day and that we ask the favor of continuing for a while receiving its support and care.

2. That we do not consider the time ripe for a separation of the Conference, since such a division would be very harmful to our church work wherefore we desire to remain with the Minnesota Conference.

3. That we as a District do not want to be partners in the agitation which is carried on in the Red River Valley, because we consider the time not distant when North Dakota ought and must have its own Conference.

4. That these resolutions be sent to the president of the Conference and published in the Minnesota *Stats Tidning.*"[14]

Thus the Red River Valley had passed through the pangs and birthpains and formed its own Conference.

A Survey

Let us look at the new Conference for a moment, as we find it pictured in the 1913 (1912) minutes. The Alexandria District which included the present Bemidji District had 43 congregations with 3,668 communicants and 2,186 children; 13 pastors, 41 churches and a total income of $34,648.00. The Fargo District had 13 congregations with 1,234 communicants and 871 children; 5 pastors, 13 churches and a total income of $12,365.00. The Red River District had 35 congregations with 1,963 communicants and 464 children, 8 pastors, 29 churches, 8 parsonages and a total income of $21,387.00.[15] This makes a total of 91 congregations with 6,865 communicants, 4,521 children, 26 pastors and 83 churches. Only two pastors had single church parishes and one of these was vice pastor of eight congregations. Nine pastors had three congregations each and four had four congregations each.

At the Diamond Jubilee of the Minnesota Conference, the president, Dr. P. A. Mattson, wrote: "We ought also to mention that in 1912 the Red River Valley Conference was organized and the following year the Canada Conference. We do not believe that the organization of these Conferences hurt the mother Conference. On the contrary we have found that the smaller Conferences can show greater results than the larger. Large bodies move more slowly than smaller ones. This is also true within the church." [16]

Even though the Red River Valley Conference has not any extraordinary or phenomenal chapters to present, it has nevertheless, at least in part, verified the above statement. It has carried on its home mission program with zeal from the very first. It has raised its budget in full even in the years of drought and depression. It has written an important chapter in Christian charity. When we take into consideration the many small sized congregations, the multiplicity of churches in the separate parishes and the average—rather humble—conditions of the people economically, the Conference has been an honor to the mother Conference and a joy to the Church at large.

The home mission has been the great task which from the beginning challenged the efforts of the new Conference.

From the very first this work was under the supervision and guidance of the Mission Board, consisting of one pastor and one layman from each District with the President and Treasurer of the Conference ex officio members. In January 1939 the Red River Valley was merged with the Minnesota Conference in the Home Mission setup and Pastor C. G. Anderson became then the Regional Director of this area. Since July 1, 1945, the Red River Valley and the Canada Conferences have been together as a Home Mission area and Dr. Anton A. Nelson is the Regional Director.

The reports from the fields are intensely interesting. Especially challenging are the needs of the smaller scattered settlements in the northern part of Minnesota. Home missionaries were sent to care for the various fields. The Conference by resolution suggested that pastors in established congregations devote some time each summer to the home mission work.[17] "In this way not only a saving of money would be made, but the pastors will get a better knowledge of the needs of the field and can better present these needs to their congregations."[18] The Conference also decided on having a home missionary superintendent.[19] In the reports we find utterances like: "The entire Bemidji District is one solid mission field." "The whole Roseau county is a large mission field. From Warren to Spooner we have much work awaiting us."[20] The president reports in 1916: "The Red River Valley Conference has 60,000 Swedes within its territory. It numbers 12,000—thus 40,000 are still outside the church. We must have men now; in a few years it will be too late. . . . We would need twelve pastors to take care of the needs within the Conference."[21] Later we find it reported officially: "A few years ago it seemed that almost all the mission fields in the northern part of the Conference were places that had rather a bright future," but he intimates that the prospects have diminished.[22] Looking back another president reports: "Our mission fields are not what they were thirty-forty years ago. The people gathered in large groups in our settlements and large congregations came into existence in a hurry. Now the missionary must travel on foot through the forests and wilderness, seeking a few families here and a few there." [23] The reasons for this change are to be found in the general financial depression, crop and bank failures and the people moving into large cities.[24]

Even where congregations were not organized the missionary efforts were not wasted. There was a sowing of the good seed. Among such places are the following: Doumas, near Red Lake; Crookston, Wadena, Nymore, Thorshult, Willow Creek, Town of Frohn, ten miles east of Itasca Park, Vern.

The pastors and congregations also looked toward the dawn of consolidation and merger of the Lutheran church. The Mission Board of this Conference and that of the Northern District of the Norwegian Lutheran Church considered the advisability to "consider the rearranging the work in certain fields." [25]

Expansion

The North Dakota District, as we have seen, asked the "favor of continuing a while" with the mother Conference— Minnesota—and expressed the hope that it would in a short time be a separate Conference. The main reason for this action was the anticipated weakness on the part of the new organization in properly caring for the large mission fields; also the confidence in the future of the prairie State. Time seemed to prove quite convincingly that the new child among the Conferences of the Augustana Synod did not only live, but was gaining strength all the time. Furthermore it seemed quite unnatural for the North Dakota delegation to cross the Red River Valley territory to reach its own meetings.

At a Home Mission Conference of all the Augustana pastors of North Dakota, held at Sheyenne, No. Dak., August 30, 1939, a discussion was held on the topic: "Should the Districts of North Dakota affiliate with the Red River Valley Conference or should they organize a North Dakota Conference?" There was considerable discussion and the consensus of opinion was that it would be best to join the Red River Valley Conference. Accordingly the following resolution was unanimously adopted and submitted to the two Districts:

> "Under existing circumstances we believe that it would be more advantageous for the churches of the Bismarck and Sheyenne Districts to belong to the Red River Valley Conference than to the Minnesota Conference.

> We therefore recommend that the Districts involved consider this matter at their next annual meetings and if favorable action be received, present the necessary petition to the Minnesota Conference and if granted by this body seek admission to the Red River Valley Conference." [26]

The Bismarck District adopted at its annual meeting at Valley City, North Dakota, February 14, 1940, and forwarded to the Minnesota Conference the following resolution:

> "The Bismarck District of the Minnesota Conference petitions said Conference for our release from her confines because of the difficult geographical problems and that we thereby might be enabled to apply for admission into the Red River Valley Conference in order that these difficulties may be solved."

The petition arrived too late to be considered by the Executive Committee and was therefore referred directly to the Conference for action. The Conference resolved,

> "That the petition from the Bismarck District be granted, provided that a similar petition in due and proper form be received from the Sheyenne District. The Executive Committee is hereby authorized to grant a release to said Sheyenne District to join the Red River Valley Conference when such a petition is presented." [27]

Meanwhile there had been considerable activity in the northern District. At its annual meeting in the Klara church, Heimdal, September 25-26, 1939, the District adopted the resolution from the Home Mission Conference, with the proviso: "That each congregation of the Sheyenne District be given the right, at its annual meetings, to fix its own pledge of Conference and Synod dues, from year to year, in accordance with the rate of such contributions, as have been allowed, while belonging to the Minnesota Conference these last years." [28]

This District decision was forwarded to the president of the Red River Valley Conference for his opinion. His answer, dated November 18, 1939, was: "It is evident to me that it would be advantageous for the North Dakota congregations to be a part of the Red River Valley Conference. Because of their location, geographically, we could serve them easier than the Minnesota Conference and our people in our congregations up here are more of the same mind, possibly, than they are in the Minnesota Conference because of a large part of that Conference being in the cities.

"However, I must say that the way the petition reads, it does not seem to me, that our Conference could grant your request at this time. I personally, feel that if you desire membership in the Red River Valley Conference you should be willing to come in unconditionally and not demand that you have the right to fix your own budget and that your budget is not to be other than you have been paying in the Minnesota Conference. It may be that your budget is more than we ask and it may be less. . . . Nor do I feel that our treatment of the smaller congregations within our Conference has been of such a nature that you should be constrained to place such demands upon us." [29]

The Bismarck District presented its petition to the Red River Valley Conference, which in turn, "resolved, that in view of the resolution by the Minnesota Conference relative to the

Bismarck District petition, action on this petition be deferred until such time as the condition of the Minnesota Conference shall have been fulfilled by the Sheyenne District, and that we express our appreciation of the action taken by the Bismarck District." [30]

At the meeting in Minot, North Dakota, September 24, 1940, it was decided to make application for admission into the Red River Valley Conference, "omitting the condition"— proviso. Therefore this petition was submitted: "Resolved that the Sheyenne District petition the Minnesota Conference to be released to join the Red River Valley Conference; Be it further resolved, that we petition the Red River Valley Conference for admission with the Bismarck District." [31]

The president of the Red River Valley Conference states in his annual message, 1941: "At our convention a year ago a petition was received from the Bismarck District of the Minnesota Conference for admission into our Conference. Because the Minnesota Conference had granted release to the Bismarck District on condition that the Sheyenne District also petition for admission into the Red River Valley Conference, action upon the petition from the Bismarck District was deferred. At this time we also have an application from the Sheyenne District and thus it becomes our duty to take action upon these petitions at this convention." [32]

The Conference resolved,
"That the petitions of the Bismarck and Sheyenne Districts of the Minnesota Conference asking for admission into the Red River Valley Conference be granted subject to the approval of the Synod." [33]

The president of the Minnesota Conference reports in 1942: "The Bismarck and Sheyenne Districts are now definitely a part of the Red River Valley Conference, being received last year." This is the only official reference made in the printed records to this separation.

The section of our church which thus became a part of this Conference included, 27 congregations with 2,347 adult members and 888 children, 23 churches and 9 parsonages. The church property was valued at $193,000. The total for the Conference was now 41 pastors, 116 congregations, 76 churches, 46 parsonages, 14,010 adult members and 5,091 children. Property value—$1,096,872.

The Red River Valley Conference has kept most of its officials in office a long period of time.

President:
    Dr. S. W. Swenson, 1912-1922
    Dr. O. O. Gustafson, 1922-1952
    Pastor Walter E. Carlson, 1952-

Vice President:
    Dr. James Moody, 1912-1918; 1921-1924
    Pastor F. M. Eckman, 1918-1921; 1924-1926
    Pastor Walfred Erickson, 1926-1943
    Pastor O. E. Clauson, 1943-1944
    Pastor Aner O. Bloom, 1944-1945
    Pastor G. W. Sandstead, 1945-1948
    Pastor Eskil Bostrom, 1948-1950
    Pastor Walter Carlson, 1950-1952
    Pastor M. Ahlstrom, 1952

Secretary:
    Pastor J. M. Persenius, 1912-1920
    Pastor O. O. Gustafson, 1920-1922
    Pastor Constant Johnson, 1922-1927
    Pastor J. Edor Larson, 1927-1930
    Pastor J. Elmer Dahlgren, 1930-1942
    Pastor G. A. Johns, 1942-

Treasurer:
    Mr. August Lundgren, 1912-1932
    Mr. Emil E. Gahlon, 1932-

References

[1] Minnesota Stats Tidning, February 15, 1905, p. 8.
[2] Ibid, January 11, 1902.
[3] Minutes, Minnesota Conference, 1909, p. 47, 48.
[4] Ibid, 1909, p. 55.
[5] Ibid, 1910, p. 107.
[6] Minutes, Alexandria District, 1910, p. 17.
[7] Krantz, J. A. Minutes, Minnesota Conference, 1912, p. 34.
[8] Minutes, R.R.V. Conference, 1913, p. 10.
[9] Ibid, p. 9.
[10] Minnesota Stats Tidning, March 22, 29, 1911. Minutes, Minnesota Conference, 1909, p. 55; 1910, p. 107.
[11] Minutes, R.R.V. Conference, Meeting in Moorhead, Minn., 1913, p. 13.
[12] Minutes, Augustana Synod, 1912, p. 21.
[13] Ibid, 1912, p. 151-153.
[14] Ibid, 1913, pp. 149-150.
[15] Ibid, 1913.
[16] Korsbaneret, 1934, p. 105.
[17] Minutes, R.R.V. Conference, 1922, p. 17; 1920, p. 15.
[18] Ibid, 1920, p. 20.
[19] Ibid, 1920, p. 29; 1927, p. 56.
This resolution was never carried out. The Conference did not have a Field Secretary of Home Mission until it arranged to have a Regional Director jointly with the Minnesota and later Canada Conferences.
[20] Ibid, 1921, p. 16; 1918, p. 19.
[21] Ibid, 1923, p. 15.
[22] Ibid, 1928, p. 14.
[23] Ibid, 1917, p. 15.
[24] Ibid, 1928, p. 14.
[25] Ibid, 1928, p. 15; 1912, p. 47; 1914, p. 38, 32.
In 1938 the Hettinger and New England fields were turned over to the E.L.C. Church.
[26] Minutes, Bismarck District, August 30, 1939, p. 105.
[27] Minutes, Minnesota Conference, 1940, p. 46.
[28] Minutes, Sheyenne District, 1939, p. 113.
[29] Ibid, p. 130 ff.
[30] Minutes, R.R.V. Conference, 1941, p. 21.
[31] Minutes, Sheyenne District, p. 133.
[32] Minutes, R.R.V. Conference, 1941, p. 21.
[33] Ibid, p. 24.

Rev. C. G. Anderson
Regional Director, 1939-1945

Dr. Anton A. Nelson
Regional Director since 1945

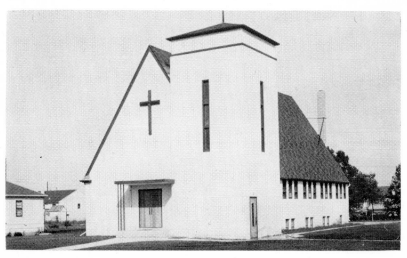

Messiah Lutheran Church, Fargo

V. DISTRICTS

The mission Districts have played a very important part in the organization, work and development of our church, especially in the early decades. From the pioneer days we read: "We can hardly speak of mission meetings in the early days. There were only two pastors out here. When the third pastor arrived we decided to have a mission meeting, but one of the pastors misunderstood the time of the meeting so he came a week too late." [1] But as soon as it was possible Districts were organized. The territory comprising the Minnesota Conference was in 1873 divided into three mission Districts, centering along the main railroads.

The Alexandria District

In the first book of Minutes we read: "That part of the Minnesota Conference which now constitutes the Alexandria District was at first exclusively a mission field. Through the missionary efforts of the Conference the first congregation on this field was organized in 1866. Pastor J. P. Lundblad was the first resident pastor in this region. Besides Parkers Prairie he also served Wadena, Fahlun, Lake Ida and Alexandria. Shortly after the arrival of Pastor Lundblad came Pastor A. Wahlin to Oscar Lake, the mother church of the District, and he also served Norunga and Wennersborg." In 1874 the workers received a needed reinforcement by the arrival of Pastor S. J. Kronberg to the northwestern part of the District in Douglas and Otter Tail counties, with Christine Lake as his place of residence. This extensive field was soon enlarged considerably when Pastor Wahlin moved to Cannon Falls and the parish he had served was added to that which Pastor Kronberg was serving. Under these conditions it was difficult to think of a District organization.

In 1876 or 1877 Pastor J. P. Mattson came to Upsala and Eksjo, Pastor L. O. Lindh to Alexandria and Pastor Louis Johnson to Oscar Lake.[2] This encouraged the pastors so that they organized the Alexandria District at the time of the installation of Pastor L. O. Lindh, in September, 1879. Pastors present were: S. J. Kronberg, L. Johnson, L. O. Lindh and the president of the Synod, Dr. E. Norelius. There were nineteen small congregations in the territory and sixteen of these reported a combined membership of 761. The majority of the congregations reported having log churches. But in size the District was full-grown from the very beginning. It was too large for the few pastors. The exact size is not easy to determine, because it had no boundaries, especially to the northwest. Through the streams of immigrants coming west it expanded so rapidly that within a very short time the entire Red River Valley and North Dakota were included.[3] Looking back a president of the Red River Valley Conference declared in his message that "in 1879 the District bordered on the east and south to the St. Paul District, west to the Pacific ocean and to the north to the White Sea."[4] Later we read: "Doumas is a small settlement near (Red) Lake and extensive swamps, which mark the northern boundary of the Alexandria District."[5] There were a total of five pastors in the District at its inception. Besides the aforementioned there were Pastors J. P. Lundblad and J. P. Mattson.

The Red River Valley is about three hundred miles in length and fifty miles in breadth. Along the edge toward the east is the Park Region territory which forms a transition from the plains to the west and the wooded sections to the east. This is the region where many of the earliest settlers founded their homes. It is interesting to notice that the early congregations were springing up, one after another in the pioneer gloom, as the yard lights in our modern day brighten the countryside in the evenings.

The first church in the Alexandria District was—as we have

noted—Oscar Lake. Three years later the Lake Ida congregation was organized by Pastor O. Beck, in 1869. Two years later six congregations were organized by Pastor J. Magney. All of these were quite close together and were in the settlements where Pastor Magney had visited and labored the most. In 1874 the Swedes who lived in the thickly forested region near Pelican Rapids organized the Central Swede Grove congregation. Pastor O. I. Kassa was the first pastor. The next year a congregation was organized at Holmes City and in 1876 Pastor Lundblad gathered the countrymen in Spruce Hill into a congregation. In 1877 Pastor P. Backman presided at the organization of the church at Alexandria. Pastor Kronberg was chairman at the initial meeting of the Fridhem congregation at Barrett the same year. The Augustana congregations at Elizabeth and Fergus Falls date back to the same year. From then on the pace was slowed up somewhat, as we notice by the following list: Zion, Amor, 1879; Bethel, Herman, 1880; Compton, 1882; Immanuel, Evansville, 1883; Zionsborg, 1884; Bethlehem, Elbow Lake, 1887; Immanuel, Clarissa, 1888; Grace, Henning, 1889; Petri, Eagle Bend and Trinity, Sebeka, 1890; Esther, Parkers Prairie, 1893; Balsamlund, Aldrich, 1894; Little Sauk, 1897; Bethel and Aeneas, Hoffman and First, Kensington, 1901; First, Miltona, 1921; Grace, Browerville, 1944.

From the pens of the pioneer pastors we learn of their travel and travail. P. Sjöblom reports that he preached in Fergus Falls two Sundays out of three and once during the week. He instructed the confirmands here and in Compton (fifty miles away). He visited White Stone Hill, North Dakota—eighty miles away—"where many countrymen have lived eight years without having had a visit by any pastor." [6] In his diary Pastor J. Magney writes: "I went to Fergus Falls to visit the honorable president of the Conference. I felt so at home in their cozy little parsonage. I also called at the home of Pastor S. J. Kronberg. He was happy and genial, as always.

He labors quietly and successfully in his parish and is well liked. August 25th I concluded the work on my assigned field by organizing a congregation in Eagle Bend. Not very many joined but those who did join were united and personally interested. The discussion was therefore not about material things, but rather about the Kingdom of God." [7]

There were trials and hardships of various kinds. Thus a pastor writes: "At the first early Christmas service it was thirty-five below zero. The church was a poorly built log house. Many of the logs were half rotten or burned in forest fires before used. The walls were poorly made, so there were big cracks between the logs. Rough boards were the ceiling, so far apart that you could put your fingers between." [8]

There were trials affecting larger areas. Thus at a Conference meeting in Marine, Minnesota, October 1877, the pastors and delegates from the "grasshopper districts" were called to meet to formulate a report on the conditions in the territory surveyed. The next day this committee reported that there were 170 families which needed immediate help. They were distributed as follows: Parkers Prairie 12, Bethania 4, Bethesda 11, Mamrelund 27, Florida 5, Nest Lake 7, Genesee 20, Swede Grove 2, Beckville 3, Tripolis 20, Swea 19, Eagle Lake 21, Christine Lake 18, Swedlanda 4. "From Norunga and Oscar Lake congregations no report has come in, but it is taken for granted there were many in need, as they have suffered from the grasshoppers several years." [9] It was resolved that the congregations which had been spared from the plague gather money for those who suffer. The following year we hear that "the physical distress which has come to many of our churches as a result of the ravages of the grasshoppers, has undoubtedly brought much distress to many, but we rejoice in that the emergency committee has been in position to extend help and has not refused any request where it was duly verified." [10]

Though the District covered a large area it was opposed to

division. Thus in 1884 it decided at a meeting in Oscar Lake that "in case the question of dividing the District is brought up at the Conference meeting we humbly petition that the matter be tabled for the time being." The same resolution was repeated the following year. May 5, 1886, the northwestern "subdistrict" petitioned for permission to organize itself into a separate District, but in answer the southwestern "subdistrict" declared that it did not consider the time ripe for such a division mainly because the "boundary lines are not 'districtly' appropriate."

At a meeting in Parkers Prairie, November 9-10, 1886, the District petitioned the Minnesota Conference for permission to divide in such a way, that the south boundaries of Clay and Becker counties constitute the District boundary line; and that the southern District retains the name Alexandria District while the northern part be known as the Red River District. In 1895 the Alexandria District asked to be relieved of the White Stone Hill and other congregations in the southeastern part of North Dakota. The following year the District notified the Pacific District that "it cannot receive the Herman congregation"—though it was later received.[11] The Alexandria District petitioned in 1916 that a division be made and the Conference recommended that "a new District be organized in the northeast part of the Red River Valley Conference, as soon as considered advisable."[12] This division took place in 1919 when the Bemidji District came into being.

Much stress was put on the mission meetings. Because of the great distances between the churches the meetings were perambulatory where the pastors conducted services in two or more places—mostly 'more' places—with one or more pastors at each place. Thus: "The next meeting shall be held in Warren and that meetings be continued in Moorhead."[13] Or "in order to lighten the work of the pastors, therefore, resolved that the District be divided into two sections, so that the western section consists of the pastors of the Elbow Lake, Christine

Lake, Eagle Lake, Fergus Falls and Elizabeth parishes; and the eastern section comprises the pastors of the Clarissa, Parkers Prairie, Fahlun, Alexandria, Holmes City and Hoffman parishes."[14] "That each of these divisions decide on their meetings and that joint meetings be held each spring, alternately in Alexandria and Fergus Falls."

The secretary was instructed to "investigate carefully the needs of the congregations and arrange and publish the programs accordingly." (1885). At each meeting one afternoon was set aside for devotional purposes among the pastors—usually lectures, Bible study and prayer. There was much concern for the success of the meetings. "The pastors shall not announce any meetings in their respective congregations to conflict with the District mission meetings."[15] The pastors were expected to attend. "If a pastor is absent three times without valid excuse his pastorate shall not receive a mission meeting that year."

It is interesting to follow the missionary endeavors of the pastors. The parishes were extensive and travel was slow and difficult. The Conference president reports that Pastor Louis Johnson had preached in Fergus Falls every third Sunday, in Compton and Peace Prairie every third Sunday and in Parkers Prairie and Esther every third. "It is hard for Pastor Johnson and his horses, but the pastor is willing and his horses must obey."[16]

The District watched its opportunities and assisted the weak and struggling congregations. It counselled faithfully and was fervent in missionary work. The Bemidji field was taken up and the work there was carried on independently on a District basis. We read: "The settlement near Hart Lake is the home mission project of the Alexandria District." This missionary project was broadened to include Bemidji, Clearbrook and other places.[17] Three years in succession the District petitioned that a pastor be called to the Park Rapids-Akely field, but without avail.

70

The District did not only petition, but it also worked. "Resolved that the president and secretary work out a schedule for the pastor's work in vacant pastorates along the Great Northern railroad, especially Park Rapids, Akely, Walker, Cass Lake, Bemidji, Bagley, Blackduck, etc., and that pastors go two and two." [18] This item is interesting: "That only one service a day be held in any regular congregation, so that more time may be allotted to the mission fields." [19] It was often a hard task that confronted the missionary. Pastor J. H. Randahl reported only ten people in the audience at the first service. In one small town he found six Swedish saloonkeepers and in many places families with several children unbaptized. But "we consider it God's special grace to be permitted to serve these regions. It is a slow task to do the pioneer work where the woods are denser than elsewhere."

The Bemidji District

We have seen the missionary efforts in the various communities in the northern woods. In 1881 the St. John's congregation at Fertile, was organized. Five years later two congregations, the Salem, McIntosh and Lima, Erskine, came into existence. The following year we have Poplar Lake congregation at Fosston and in 1889 the Asphult congregation at Fosston, and Oak Park. Then there is a period of nineteen years during which there were no new congregations. Instead the missionary efforts must have been shifted to other places since during this period six congregations were organized in the southern part of the Alexandria District, five in the Fargo District, fifteen in the Red River District and seven in North Dakota. In 1908 the Bethel church, Bemidji, Capernaum, Blackduck and Zion, Cass Lake were born. Then follow Augustana, Clearbrook, 1910; Fridhem, Lengby, 1911; while the youngest in the family of churches are First, Hines, 1915, and Zion, Leonard, 1916. One reason for the rather slow expansion of the church in these regions may be found in the relatively slow pace of settlement where the forests were dense and clearing the land was therefore difficult. The organization of congregations was the result of arduous and consecrated missionary efforts by the pastors and laymen.

The Alexandria District with its large territory and its forty-five congregations found it advisable to divide. The president of the Conference, Dr. S. W. Swenson, mentions in his annual report to the Convention at Warren, Minnesota, May 21-25, 1919, that "the brethren of the Alexandria District are petitioning to be permitted to form a new District under the name of the Bemidji District. This petition should be granted since the Alexandria District is too large and cumbersome to work as it is. The Red River District is also too large to serve because of the great distances and the many congregations. The Fargo District is of right size and easy to take care of." [20]

Though the official minutes make no mention of the fact, the petition was granted by the Conference since the 1920 Minutes include statistics of the Bemidji District—12 congregations with 604 adults and 436 children, four pastors, and a property value of $30,000.

The Fargo and North Dakota Districts

The first Augustana congregation in the State of North Dakota was Maple Sheyenne, thirteen miles north of Fargo, organized by Pastor A. P. Monten in 1878. Pastor Monten made a missionary trip through this region at the request of the Conference. Pastor S. A. Lindholm, serving the Bethesda Church in Moorhead, also conducted services in Fargo. The meetings were held in the front part of the Peterson Feed Store, corner of Broadway and Fourth Avenue, then known as the Ely Block. It was not until 1891 that the Elim congregation at Fargo was organized. A correspondent writes later that the Swedish Lutheran congregation "owns a small, tasteful church and gives every evidence of intending to live. Had it been organized ten years earlier it would undoubtedly be self-supporting by now," (1896). "During the time which elapsed other communions, Swedish and American Lodges, and the habit of living without God have caused many of our people to be inaccessible to Lutheran Christendom." [21]

From Moorhead a "beach-head" was made at the capital of North Dakota. In 1881 the Minnesota Conference offered to support the Bethesda church at Moorhead with $300 on condition that its pastor, J. O. Cavallin, be permitted to make three trips into North Dakota.[22] The result was the organization of the First Lutheran Church, Bismarck. Pastor J. P. Sward made a trip to Bismark in 1884. In the latter part of that same year Pastor E. J. Werner was there. "I found the congregation, not quite two years old, in good condition. A Christian and church spirit was there. The membership is still small, only 25 communicants, but it will greatly increase because of immigration." [23] He reported to the Conference meeting in February, 1885, that the church at Bismarck had acquired a property in the beautiful part of the city and had erected a parsonage which also was used as a place of worship.[24] "In Bismarck the services are well attended by young and old and many seem to love to hear the Word." [25] Pastor Werner also visited Painted Woods, fifteen or twenty miles north of Bismarck and preached daily for two weeks "in their low and primitive hovels." [26] A congregation was organized there November 18, 1884, but we have no records of it after 1895. Students Theo. Kjellgren and A. A. Westin were in Bismarck in 1885; Pastors Cavallin and L. J. Lundquist in 1886. Pastor S. A. Lindholm reports in 1886 that most of his time had been spent in Bismarck, Slaughter and neighborhood. Pastors J. E. Shipp and Aug. A. Nelson also worked there during summer vacations. "The work in North Dakota is still in its infancy," we read. "One of the hindrances is that the people are so scattered." [27]

"Pastor S. Udden," we read, "has put forth most efforts in Barnes and Steele counties, has visited Casselton, Jamestown and Sheyenne where many Swedes live." [28] That was in 1880. Nine years later we find him working in the south part of Polk county where he made five visits. There were three congregations and many mission fields.[29] Pastor Sjoblom reports to the Conference in 1890: "The first place which I visited was Oakes, North Dakota. In this city, and even more so in the country in all directions is said to be many Swedes. We should have a pastor stationed here." [30] Not until fifteen years later was there a congregation at Oakes.—"About forty people were gathered in the public schoolhouse in Jamestown. Had we had a congregation here eight or ten years ago it would have been large by this time." [31] A congregation was organized in Valley City June 24, 1895. "It might have had a much larger membership (than 39 communicants) if the Synod had not adhered so strictly to the conservative position relative to secret orders. Even here the tempter may cast his snare over the necks of many." [32] A correspondent declares that "the Swedes own relatively little property in the Dakotas." [33]

Here are a few glimpses from the mission fields in North Dakota during the formative period. "Out here on the prairies the Christmas festival is observed in the customary way. Early Christmas morning the people of the Elmdale congregation west of Kenmare gathered for morning service. In spite of the bitter cold many attended. We met again in the afternoon. Wednesday evening the Immanuel church, near McKinney, had its children's festival. New Year's Day two services were conducted in the Swedish settlement west of Flaxton." [34] "The entire Christmas season was one continuous period of festivities because we had services every day. It is truly encouraging for a pastor when the people are willing to drive many miles day after day to attend." [35]

This vast territory was first a part of the Alexandria District. In 1898 a petition was presented to the Minnesota Conference that the District be divided and as a result three Districts were formed:

A. The Central District comprising Norman, Becker and Clay counties in Minnesota, and Cass county in North Dakota.

B. The Red River District including Roseau, Kittson, Marshall, Red Lake and Polk counties, Minnesota and Grand Forks county, North Dakota.

C. The James River District covering all parts of North Dakota except Grand Forks and Cass counties.

When this decision had been made a meeting was held in Fargo and Moorhead to arrange the affairs of the new Districts. First there was the business they had in common. Mr. J. P. Dahlquist was remunerated for his work in and around Roseau. Twenty-five dollars was appropriated for the work in Roseau, "after which this important mission be given to the Red River District"; and the "attention of the Conference was called to the need of forming parishes and supplying workers."[36] The congregations were reminded of a resolution that an offering be lifted to help the Bethesda church in Marshall county, "which has a large indebtedness on its church." Finally it was decided to divide the money in the treasury—$12.28 —equally between the three Districts. Thereupon it was decided that Pastor J. A. Nyvall should convene the Central District, Pastor L. P. Lundberg the Red River, and Pastor O. J. Andrews the James River District. Adds the secretary of the former united District: "Then the District adjourned, conscious of its gratitude to God for His guidance and blessing in the past, to the brethren who in the past and present in humility, patience and sacrifice have labored for the extension of the Kingdom of God. May the cordial spirit which has characterized the former District, we pray, continue among the brethren of the new organizations." [37]

In 1909 the North Dakota (James River) District was divided into two: 1. The North Dakota District comprising all the congregations, except Eksjo, Detroit Lakes, Moorhead, Fargo, Maple, Sheyenne and Crookston, which were: 2. The Fargo District.[38]

The next change came January 25-27, 1916, when after "a thorough discussion" a petition was adopted asking for a division of the North Dakota District so that Hofva, Finley; White Stone Hills; Nebo, Valley City; Maris, Braddock; Sunne, Wilton; Vasa, Litchville; Salem, Oakes; Bethel, Malcolm; Birka, Basto; Gustavus Adolphus, Gwinner; Augustana, Underwood; Lebanon, Rainy Butte; Saron, Midway; Salem, Flasher and missions, be the southern—Bismarck—District; and that Augustana, Sheyenne, Klara, Maddock; Sion, Souris; Tolley; Elmdale, Niobe; Elim, Bergen; Bethania, Lignite; Minot; Antler; Bethania, Glenburn; Herman, Plummer; Messiah, Greene; Vasa, Fish Lake; Bethel, Ray, and missions be the northern—Sheyenne—District.[39]

The petition was granted by the Conference and the pastors and delegates from North Dakota gathered in the Augustana church, Minneapolis, February 28, 1916—during the Conference Convention—to organize the two Districts. Pastor N. P. Tuleen, president, expressed the "hope and prayer that both the new Districts might labor for the advancement of the Kingdom of God. Then the north and the south—Sheyenne and Bismarck—took a cordial farewell of each other and met separately for organization." [40]

At a meeting of the Red River Valley Conference in Parkers Prairie, Minnesota, May 1942, a petition was presented that some of the congregations of the Bismarck District might join the Fargo District. A committee was elected to study the matter and in accordance with the recommendation of this committee the parishes of Valley City, Oakes and Gwinner became members of the Fargo District. In October 1943 the pastors of the remaining congregations of the Bismarck District asked to join the Sheyenne District. The Conference gave its sanction at the meeting in Warren, Minnesota, 1944. Thus came into existence the present North Dakota District.

Having sketched the historical development of these Districts we want to notice a few characteristics. The work of the church presented problems somewhat peculiar to this particular area. Because of the great distances the pastors were quite isolated. Asks a president, referring to the difficulty of getting pastors: "Is the Sheyenne District to be classified among the rocky fields of the Augustana Synod? Are the pastors afraid that they may not be supported financially?" [41] It may be reported as a possibly exceptional occurrence that all the pastors of a District would arrive in the same year; but such was the case in North Dakota in 1910. Pastor C. W. Samuelson was still at Oakes, but had resigned. Pastor Cavallin arranged for the installation of the new pastors. Pastors J. A. Krantz, J. Theo. Kjellgren and S. A. Lindholm made an apostolic trip through the District, November 14-22. Dr. Krantz installed Pastor C. O. Gulleen in Souris and Pastor J. E. Liljedahl in Valley City, while Pastor Kjellgren installed Pastor N. P. Tuleen in Sheyenne and Pastor E. F. Alfson in Bismarck.[42]

There were trials and difficulties. Some were the same as those experienced elsewhere. "There would be greater growth if it were not for the sects, worldliness and indifference." [43] There were difficulties of travel. "How the rest got to Klara I do not know, but we who came from the north had an adventurous trip on bad roads. We were stuck time and time again, fought mosquitoes, sweated, read *Lindsborgsposten* and discovered new methods of getting out of the mud." [44] "The next morning we started out for Antler. Everything went well until we caught up with a lumber wagon and stopped to ask the way. The Overland did not stop soon enough and hit the wagon, causing several leaks in the radiator. At first we stood dumbfounded with despair written on our faces, but presently we resolutely began to hammer out the buckles and shove rags in the holes. With a pail along for emergency we started slowly for town." [45] Or we have the contrast: "Pastor Edward Ekstrom walked from New Rockford to Sheyenne — eleven miles—and saved the District fifty cents."[46] "The pastors arrived at midnight. The rain and snow played havoc with our mission meetings this time." [47] "At nine a.m. we came to a waterpool where two cars were stuck. We turned around and found lodging with Melvin Kopang. Sleeping quarters for the three pastors were found in the haymow. In the morning Mr. Kopang loaned us a team so we made our way to the school house."[48] Comments the secretary: "Whoever reads this may understand that such a missionary journey is toilsome and tedious, since one must preach two or three times a day and travel between places during the time one normally should sleep and rest." [49]

At a meeting in Hobart, North Dakota, dinner was served "in the church barns." When the minutes were read at the following meeting Dr. J. A. Krantz was present and asked: "Var va de andra kräka då?" (Where were then the other creatures?), to which the secretary replied: "De va utanför." (They were outside.) The secretary adds that the barns were new and had not been used.[50]

The District reports are very interesting. The pastors looked at times and conditions very realistically. "Disastrous floods and droughts of alarming dimensions have been destroying property valued in the billions of dollars. Along the vista of life we visualize people poverty-stricken, and yet not poor in spirit, millions of unemployed who live on income from government work or dole, and yet great masses stand idle in the marketplace, not willing to enter into the Lord's vineyard. In addition to the many other horrifying problems we have the liquor traffic to contend with. . . . The way out? . . . A movement back to God when young and old assemble at the cross and become imbued with the Spirit of Christ." [51]

The mission meetings of the North Dakota District would

deserve a special chapter. They were held according to the apostolic pattern, the pastors covering the entire District, traveling and preaching continuously for a period of three weeks, the distances covered were often up to eight hundred miles each tour.

Someone may say—strenuous days! Seventeen days traveling! The writer was along on some of them and he says: "Give us more of them. Give us again the days when people will gather on week days in churches and schoolhouses to hear the Word of God." The pastors travelled by train, horse or model-T Ford. The people came by team, auto or on foot. "Not only those who live near, but even those who live ten, fifteen, yes, even thirty miles away, came to the services." [52] How can I ever forget the rugged country between Mandan and Flasher, North Dakota, where we drove over or around the hills—on roads, trails or neither. How can I forget the cordial hospitality of the people. We even had "short dinner speeches" at the lunch hour on such subjects as home, church, community.[53] How could I ever forget that service in Smith's schoolhouse near Kulm that weekday afternoon when the room was packed and people were standing outside every window listening. We thought we heard the soft breezes of the Spirit of God, we seemed to hear the angels sing. The secretary closes his account of one of these journeys thus: "The result of the labors only God knows; but the bright day of eternity shall reveal, not only that the pastors of the District have struggled in prayer as Jacob, but that their prayers were heard, their work crowned with success, and through the merits of Christ they have been instrumental in leading souls to Christ." [54] Again we read: "Thus reads the schematic chronicle and we think it is only an enumeration of dates and names. But these are only the external aspects and there is another side. The outward description is merely the bark on the tree of life which has flourished in the Word spoken and sung. We hope and pray that the Kingdom of God has been advanced both among the pastors and the people. There are indications that to some these meetings have been occasions of spiritual rest, to others they have been moments when the Savior has been especially calling."[55]

The Red River District

As we have already noted, the Red River Valley District came into being November 1886, and received additional territory in 1898. On both occasions the Alexandria District was sharing from its ever expanding domain. It comprised the northwestern part of the State of Minnesota and is largely located within the famous valley. A veteran pastor writes: "The report of the fertility is now a proven reality as any one can see who travels along the River in harvest time. One is amazed to see the waving grain fields and the well built farms. . . . The Swedes who came to this area were churchly and it did not take long until Swedish Lutheran congregations were organized." [56]

The first congregation in this region was the Black River Church, near St. Hilaire, Minnesota. Pastor J. G. Lagerstrom organized it September 24, 1881. Fourteen days later he organized the Red River congregation. Simultaneously Pastor L. A. Hocanzon organized the congregation at Warren. A few miles east of Hallock was another small settlement of Swedes and Pastor Hocanzon organized a congregation there in 1883. Six years later disagreement concerning a cemetery caused some members to withdraw. Pastor Hocanzon also organized the Salem congregation near Stephen.

A congregation—Emmaus—was organized east of Kennedy in 1884 by a layman named Brown. Later when it was to be incorporated it was discovered that it had not been legally organized. A meeting was held September 24, 1896, to decide on incorporation, but some of the members in the eastern section refused to join and organized their own congregation, Octo-

80

J. Magney
1842-1910

L. A. Hocanzon
1837-1919

L. Johnson
1838-1912

J. P. Lundblad
1829-1900

P. Sjöblom
1834-1909

S. J. Kronberg
1840-1925

ber 30, 1896. As a result there were two congregations—one in Tegner Township and one in Jupiter Township—with churches only two miles apart, East and West Emmaus. On Christmas Day, 1950, the West Emmaus church burned to the ground and the members joined neighboring churches. The Tärna congregation near St. Hilaire was organized by Pastor S. Udden in 1885. The same year a congregation was organized about twenty miles from Warren and was named Hebron. Student C. A. Lindahl organized the Salem church, McIntosh and New Sweden. The following year the Bethesda church near Grand Forks came into existence. North of Thief River Falls the people organized the Park Ridge congregation in 1887, which later moved into Thief River Falls and joined the First church there.

In the "Thirteen Town" territory is a lake named Poplar Lake and the settlers in this neighborhood organized (by Pastor J. P. Lundblad) a congregation—in 1887—and named it after the lake.[57] The Swedes in the Hill River settlement, near Fosston, organized the Asphult congregation in 1889. The next year the Nyed congregation near Argyle was organized. Pastor N. J. Sture presided. The following year the Immanuel church, ten miles northwest of Warren, was organized and two years later the Elim church was formed by the Swedes living on Snake River.

In Red Lake county (then called Polk) the Oak Park congregation was organized in 1889. The Maria church, Kennedy, dates back to 1893 and the following year we have the Bethesda church, Strandquist, the Nyskoga—seventeen miles east of Grand Forks—and the Clara church, Hazel, Minnesota. In 1896 the Gustaf Adolph church, Marshall county, was organized and the following year the congregation at Grand Forks with the same name. The latter has changed the name to Augustana.[58]

Next we move into Roseau county where Pastor L. P. Lundgren in 1898 organized the Clara and Rosenlund congregations while Pastor A. Mattson organized the Betania church, Badger. The Sikar church, fourteen miles east of Hallock, was organized the same year as was also the Zion church, Bronson, Minnesota.

Pastor H. O. Hemming visited the settlements near the Lake of the Woods. A congregation—Sion—was organized in Warroad in 1904. The following year the Bloomwood congregation, ten miles west of Argyle, was organized and in 1907 the Bethlehem east of Karlstad was organized. The same year the members of the Hallock and Red River churches organized into a separate church—Tabitha.

The early years as well as later periods are described in the words of a Conference president: "The Red River District with its many small congregations is one great solid mission field."[59] And the description of the Willow Creek settlement may well be applied to larger areas: "The congregation consists of poor settlers, but they are homeloving and hospitable people, much interested in the work of the church." [60]

Pastor James Moody, one of the pioneer pastors, writes reminiscently: "In 1888 I came as a new pastor to St. Hilaire. A part of the Indian reservation had been opened for white settlers a few years before. The Thirteen Towns (Townships) around Fosston were then taken up by homesteaders. The railroad from Crookston to Fosston opened for traffic in the fall of 1888 and I was asked to do some church work around Fosston, besides my work in Crookston, Black River, St. Hilaire and Park River (Thief River Falls), which was my regular field. I got six extra preaching places, which now constitute half of the Bemidji District."

"In 1893 more of the reservation was opened for settlers and a railroad was laid out. After that I heard much about Roseau county when it was taken up by homesteaders. Their nearest railroad station was then Stephen, about fifty to seventy miles away."

"Rev. A. Hoorn had done some work in Salol and he wanted me to take charge of that field. There was no church as yet. A lady by the name of Valberg had a restaurant there and was much interested in the work of the church. She called the people together in her restaurant for divine services. After some preliminary work we decided to organize a church."[61]

We move a little farther north and listen to another pioneer pastor. "The road between Roseau and Warroad was in poor condition. It was a long day's drive in mud, water and swampy places to travel the thirty miles. I sometimes walked the entire distance rather than to drive. After services on Sunday a man asked me to come and baptize his child. I was also invited for dinner. I told him there was to be a mission meeting at Warroad and I was to be there the next day. He promised to take me a good part of the way toward Roseau, so I went with him. He kept his promise, but still I had about ten or twelve miles to walk. The night was dark. I could not see the road, but felt it with my feet. Then at a distance of about two and a half miles two timber wolves began to howl and I was frightened. Then the thought came to me: 'Den Gud bevarar är utan fara' (He whom God protects is out of danger)." [62]

A couple of curious items may be quoted from the records. Thus "the retiring president was thanked by standing up." [63] In one church where a congregation worshiped temporarily there were two organs, "One Norwegian and one Swedish. Pastor Ekstrom used the Norwegian." [64]

References

[1] Minutes, Alexandria District, p. 1.
[2] Ibid, p. 5.
[3] Ibid, p. 1.
[4] Minutes, R.R.V. Conference, 1915, p. 11.
[5] Ibid, 1916, p. 24.
[6] Minutes, Minnesota Conference, 1889, p. 32.
[7] Skaffaren, October 1, 1890.
[8] Korsbaneret, 1906, p. 92.
[9] Minutes, Minnesota Conference, MSS, p. 152.
[10] Ibid, p. 166. S. J. Kronberg has a very interesting description of the grasshopper plague. "These 'armies' of the Lord worked at his command and direction. In most places they were not permitted to take more than

that the family had enough for its needs." One farmer had a large field of wheat ready to harvest. When the first hoppers came he rushed out the binder, but when he had made a few rounds the insects had finished the whole field. Another time a swarm of hoppers settled on a five acre field and sat there all day without doing any damage. Then they flew away and settled on an oats-field where they devoured all the weeds, but did not touch the grain. See "Banbrytaren," p. 238.

11 Minutes, Alexandria District, p. 17.

12 Minutes, Minnesota Conference, 1916, p. 29.

13 Minutes, Alexandria District. Resolution adopted at meeting in Oscar Lake, 1880.

14 Larson, J. Edor, History of Alexandria District, Minutes R.R.V. Conference, 1930, p. 99.

15 Ibid, p. 101. This disciplinary measure seems to have failed at times, because the president of the District is instructed to confer with a "delinquent" pastor. Nor did this have the desired result, for the next year (1893), the president is to write to the deacons and inquire why the pastor was absent from the meetings. The next year the same pastor is admonished to attend, but the fourth year the officers of the District are asked to investigate why he does not attend.

16 Minutes, Minnesota Conference, 1895, p. 30.

17 Minutes, R.R.V. Conference, 1916, p. 23.

18 Larson, J. Edor, History Alexandria District, p. 101.

19 Ibid, p. 101.

20 Minutes, R.R.V. Conference, 1919, p. 18.

21 Minnesota Stats Tidning, January 22, 1896.

22 Lund, Dr. Emil, Minnesota konferensens historia, p. 1175.

23 Minutes, Minnesota Conference, 1896, p. 24.

24 Ibid, 1884, p. 25.

25 Ibid, 1893, p. 43. Lund, p. 1175.

26 Lund, p. 1176.

27 Minutes, Minnesota Conference, 1896, p. 24.

28 Ibid, 1880, p. 38.

29 Ibid, 1889, p. 32.

30 Ibid, 1890, p. 24.

31 Skaffaren, December 12, 1894.

32 Ibid, July 10, 1895.

33 Ibid, January 6, 1894.

34 Minnesota Stats Tidning, January 25, 1905.

35 Ibid, February 1, 1905.

36 Minutes, James River District, p. 2.

37 Ibid, p. 3.

38 Minutes, Minnesota Conference,1909,p. 132.

39 Minutes, North Dakota District, p. 139 ff.

40 Ibid, p. 2.

41 Minutes, Sheyenne District, p. 174.

42 Ibid, p. 174.

43 Ibid, p. 18.

44 Ibid, p. 4.

45 Ibid, p. 5.

46 Ibid, p. 117.

47 Ibid, p. 299.

48 Ibid, p. 94.

49 Ibid, p. 39.

50 Minutes, Bismarck District, p. 41.

51 Minutes, Sheyenne District, p. 284.

52 Minutes, Bismarck District, p. 25.

53 Ibid, p. 71.

54 Ibid, p. 15.

55 Ibid, p. 94.

56 Lundgren, L. P., Minnesskrift, p. 187.

57 "Thirteen Towns" is the name applied to thirteen Townships opened as homestead settlements in 1883. See Minnesota Stats Tidning, March 13, 1896.

84

[58] Lundgren, L. P., Minnesskrift, p. 187.
[59] Minutes, R.R.V. Conference, 1913, p. 39.
[60] Ibid, 1914, p. 30.
[61] Moody, J., Greeting to Church, Roseau. 1940.
[62] Hemming, H. O., Letter to Zion church, Warroad, at Anniversary, 1939.
[63] Minutes, Sheyenne District, 1920.
[64] Ibid, p. 113.

From April, 1924, until May, 1928, the Red River District published an eight page church paper called "Our Church." It brought news from the church in general and carried a special division called "Echoes from Our Congregations" with reports and news from the individual congregations.

VI. CHRISTIAN EDUCATION

It has been stated that the main reason the Lutheran churches in the early Delaware colony were lost was the fact that no
provisions were made for Christian education and the training
of pastors. In contrast we marvel at the foresight, the interest
and the ability of the church of the northwest pioneers in the
nineteenth century to plan and carry out educational projects.
The section of our church which is now the Red River Valley
Conference has had not less than four schools.

Hope Academy, 1888-1896

We are told that Dr. E. Norelius at one time (1882) planned
to locate in Moorhead in order to promote the school project.
The matter of establishing a school was discussed at a meeting
held in August, 1882.[1] The plan was to begin with an ordinary
parochial school, but add new courses until it gradually would
develop into a college. As the boom in and around Moorhead
subsided the idea of a school likewise began to wane. However,
some of the members of the Bethesda church, spurred on by
their pastor, were interested and at a meeting in Lake Park,
1887, "The Lutheran Benevolent Society" was organized. In
February, 1888, the Society met to "consider the expediency of
establishing an educational institution somewhere in the Red
River Valley. After prayerful deliberations and a full survey
of the situation, it was unanimously decided to locate the Academy in Moorhead, if sufficient encouragement would be offered by its citizens and by the people in other parts of the
Red River Valley. Generous contributions were made by
many and on the first day of November the same year, the
Academy was opened. On the very same day the Society met
and adopted its Articles of Incorporation."[2]

One of the most enthusiastic workers and supporters of Hope Academy was John L. Bjorkquist, who with Pastor J. O. Cavallin, was greatly instrumental in founding the institution. His liberal donation of $2,500 which was paid in $3,000 alone made it possible to buy, during the summer of 1888, the building which served so well.[3] The school building is described as "large and commodious—partly four and partly three stories high—located in the northeastern part of the city. A large dining hall seventy-two by fifteen is on the first floor. On the second floor are the classrooms, the library and the museum; on the third the office and sixteen rooms for students. The entire building is steam heated."[4] A correspondent ("W") describes the building facilities: "I was looking for a shanty, being familiar with the Swedish valley (Svenska dalen) in St. Paul and the Gustavus Adolphus striving up the College Hill. I was surprised to find a four story building. . . . I discovered that a school can pay its way and make money even the first year. Hope Academy with its excellent location, its aspiring teachers and its good beginning has, without doubt, a glorious future."[5] We also read that "the Board of Directors have authorized the business manager, J. L. Bjorkquist, to rent two houses near the school, which shall be used as dormitories for girls."[6] Again: "The rooms are light and pleasant. The recitation rooms are agreeable and attractive. The teachers are young and energetic men and women who do everything possible that the stay of the students at the school may be enjoyable and profitable."[7]

There were four courses offered:

The Scientific—to give the young a practical knowledge for a general way of living.

The Classical—preparation for College. The chief subjects of this course were mathematics, Latin, German.

The Musical—included organ, piano, vocal and two general subjects.

The Special English Course—for those who want to learn the language, especially those of advanced age. Hope Academy was the first Swedish-American school to have such a course.

As to the aim and purpose, the "institution is sincerely Christian in character and its aim is to prepare young men and women for life under the avowed principles and influences of Christianity. Its courses are designed to furnish the elements of a solid education. It offers no substitute for earnest study and presents no inducement to those content with superficial knowledge." [8] "The discipline is not adapted to boys and girls that require severe restrictions, but to those who are willing to submit cheerfully to the wholesome restraint found necessary for the efficiency and reputation of the school." [9] Again we are told that the "Blessings that Christianity has secured for us, Christianity alone will preserve and that mainly through the upbuilding of individual character. Not upon the shifting sands of indifference and doubt, but upon the firm rock of Christian faith must that character be grounded." [10]

The Academy was sponsored by the Lutheran Benevolent Society. The 1892-3 catalogue informs us that "for five years this Society has carried on its work in a very encouraging manner; not less than 587 students having been in attendance." In the fall of 1892 it was thought that the institution could better fill the needs of its constituents by being placed under the control of the Lutheran church. A meeting was held in Moorhead on the 7th of December for the purpose of effecting a change in this direction. The result was the organization of the Red River District of the Minnesota Conference as a corporate body. This organization owned and controlled the institution. [11]

Pastor J. O. Cavallin, who had been the moving spirit in the project, became the first Principal with Samuel Challman —a graduate of Augustana College, "a born teacher, a strict disciplinarian and a consecrated Christian"—assistant Principal. From the Press we learn that Pastor H. Riggers, who came from the Mission Institute Hermansburg, Germany, also graduate of the Wartburg Seminary, Dubuque, Iowa, was "called as teacher of German language." . . . Pastor S. G. Swenson from Hallock, Minnesota, became a teacher and his credentials were good from the very start. "His work as superintendent of schools has been characterized by impartiality and conscientiousness and the schools have made great advances under his guidance."[12] Another item tells us that "six new teachers have been employed and a seventh is soon to be called. Three of the teachers have graduated from Augustana College, one has completed the business course at Gustavus Adolphus College, one came from Karlstad College, Sweden, and one from Wartburg Seminary."[13]

In 1892 the school had a library of four hundred books and pamphlets, the reading room contained about forty newspapers, the museum had a few specimens of animals, some Indian relics, some petrifications and a small numismatical collection.[14]

The Star Lyceum Literary Society was organized 1888 and four years later it reported one hundred and fifty members. It met every Friday evening for programs of debates, recitations, essays and orations. At the morning prayers and Sunday worship services attendance was compulsory. Prayer meetings were held Saturday evenings.[15] An Endowment Fund for the chair of Christianity was established and was named "The Campanius Fund" in honor of John Campanius, the Swedish Lutheran pastor, who arrived in America in 1643, dedicated the first Swedish church in America, founded one of the first Indian missions and translated the first book—Luther's Small Catechism—into the language of the Delaware Indians. The Fargo Argus has this to say about the school across the River: "A glance at the school life at this institution will assure everyone that diligence is one of the characteristics both of students and teachers. Ample assignments are given each one and punctual completion of the work is required."

The attendance the second year was one hundred and fourteen and it kept around the hundred mark most of the time. Most of the students had Scandinavian names, though there was a Calmer, Brendemuch, Rinan, Kennedy, Boatman, Linton, Scott, etc.

The expenses varied some, but 1895 may be taken as an example. Matriculation fee, $3.00; tuition, first term $9.00, second term $18.00; room $.50 per week. Each room was furnished with bedstead, commode, table and three chairs. Students furnished bedding, toilet articles and lamp. Oil was fifteen cents a gallon. Board was $2.25 a week.

At least part of the time there was a "local Board of Managers." Thus in 1893 this Board consisted of Pastor S. A. Lindholm, J. P. Dahlquist, Fargo; S. E. Eastland, L. Johnson and C. W. Freeman of Moorhead.

Writes Mrs. Chas. L. Anderson: "Kling (L. W.) did wonders with the chorus. Performance was of high order. At one concert Rupert's orchestra from Fargo was engaged. The chorus sang "Psalms of David" by Wennerberg in the Swedish. It also rendered parts of Handel's "Messiah." [16]

A correspondent describes a commencement program as being "too rich— hoc est—too long. Dr. C. J. Petri was the speaker, but it was nearly midnight before his turn came. He left his manuscript in his pocket and spoke extemporaneously but appropriately on American education." [17]

However, the institution became the victim of the times. It prospered until the crisis in 1893 and on. Even then a correspondent writes optimistically: "The creditors need only have a little patience and the one thing as well as the other shall come out all right." That was in 1894.[18] The following year another pen writes: "The bright side is Hope Academy.

We hope that when it opens its doors, October 15, several hundred students may come." [19] Again: "Hope Academy seems to be the plant of hope which shoots forth twigs and branches even though many parasites attempt to hamper its growth." [20] But the times and circumstances in this uncertain world have a habit of dashing even the fondest hopes mercilessly to the ground and mere optimism cannot save an institution.

The supporting congregations were small and a large number were vacant. Consequently the school closed its doors in 1896. Its life was brief, but while Hope Academy lived it lived well, performed a heroic service in the church and in the Kingdom of God. It may well be said that the Concordia College in Moorhead, as Elisha of old, caught the mantle of Elijah in the school of prophets.

Lund Academy, 1899-1901

While Hope Academy was drawing its last breath in death in the Red River District, the thought of a school began to make itself felt in the Alexandria District.

Pastor S. J. Kronberg was very much concerned about Christian education. He says that it was an urge which could not be suppressed. He went to God in prayer, but the obstacles seemed insurmountable. "We prayed and wept, but there seemed to be no way out." [21] The matter was discussed in smaller groups and in public, but there was no definite action. Kronberg then sent a questionnaire to the pastors and leading laymen within a radius of twenty-five or thirty miles. Five questions were submitted:

1. Do you think that a Christian school of higher learning in this District or elsewhere in the northwest is desirable and necessary?

2. Do you think such a school could be established and operated without going into debt?

3. Do you think that Christianity and the mother tongue are of primary or secondary importance?

4. Where do you think such a school should be located—in Alexandria or Fergus Falls?

5. Are you interested to the extent that you will help to promote the project?

All the persons to whom the questionnaire was directed replied, except one. The question had also been asked, if they were willing to meet in Christine Lake to discuss this matter.

A meeting was held, but nothing definite came out of it. Pastor Kronberg determined to make an attempt of his own. The schoolroom was the sacristy of the church in Christine Lake. Mr. V. E. Holmstedt, graduate of Gustavus Adolphus College—later pastor—was called as teacher.

Lund Academy was in operation for a period of ten months during two years, 1900 and 1901. There were twenty-five students. Tuition was $2.50 per month. The entire Lund Academy enterprise was an avowed experiment to demonstrate "that a school can be self-supporting." [22]

Northwestern College, 1900-1932

In the first catalogue issued by the Northwestern College we are informed, that the school was founded in 1900 and formally opened January 3, 1901. The incorporators were: John Anderson, Evansville; C. J. Enstrom, L. P. Holmquist, Pastor L. Johnson, Prof. A. C. Youngdahl, all of Fergus Falls; Pastor S. J. Kronberg, Melby; Pastor J. Moody, Martin Nelson, Battle Lake; S. J. Nylander, Amor; August Nygren, Pastor L. P. Stenstrom, Elizabeth; P. P. Setterlund, Barrett. Instructors were: A. C. Youngdahl, Principal; Clara Olson, Anton Quello, W. L. Tambling, Mabel Vaughn.

There was a great deal of preliminary discussion on the school question prior to the establishment of this institution.

The president of the District argued that very few students attended Gustavus Adolphus College from this District wherefore the congregations in this part of the Conference should not be taxed the same as the larger one near the center.[23] A correspondent writes, that "if we use good sense this question can be solved without bullets and gunpowder. We cannot blame the supporters of N. W. College if they are disappointed to see their school ignored and not even recognized by the church at large." [24]

The question was naturally discussed a great deal within the Alexandria District where the cause had many champions. Finally a resolution was adopted: "Inasmuch as the District is aware of the importance of Evangelical Lutheran education and whereas our church has no institution of higher learning north of St. Peter, Minnesota, it (the District) recommends that a corporation be formed for the establishment of a Christian Academy within the District and that the school shall begin this fall in rented quarters, either in Alexandria or Fergus Falls, if possible." [25] There was much competition between Alexandria and Fergus Falls as to site, but Fergus Falls won out.[26] Reading again from the first catalogue we find that "after three years of careful deliberations it was finally located in Fergus Falls, and through the munificent gift by Hon. J. B. Cutler of a block of land, the College has a most imposing location on a hill about a mile from the center of the city."[27] Even so it was an arduous task to establish this school. It was very dry during the early part of 1900 and the crops were therefore quite meager. Opposition from Alexandria also hampered the work.[28]

Northwestern College was "located on the banks of the Red River of the north in the so-called Park Region, one of the most beautiful parts of Minnesota. The city itself as well as the surrounding country has a predominantly Scandinavian population. There are seven Lutheran churches. While primarily a city of homes, it is nevertheless a very busy place with factories, mills and well equipped stores." [29] We are also reminded that the River, which passes through the city, has over eighty feet fall within the city limits, thus furnishing good drainage and making it a healthful location.

The first school building was seventy-six by forty-four in size, built of "hard burnt" brick, three stories high beside basement. It was modern in heating, light and water. On the first floor was the office of the principal and five classrooms, accommodating about two hundred students.[30] The attendance the first year was sixty-five. Already the second year there was an evident need for enlarged facilities. Therefore in 1902 additional land was bought and a building eighty-eight by forty, three stories high, was constructed. Mr. J. J. Hill, the railroad magnate, offered to give a donation of $4,000 provided the constituency of the school raised $6,000. The provision was met very promptly, so that the cornerstone for the new building was laid in June 1903 and the structure was ready for occupancy in the early part of 1904.[31]

The Northwestern College was owned and operated by a corporation whose members all belonged to the Evangelical Lutheran Augustana Synod. The government of the institution was vested in the Board Trustees, the Faculty and the Principal.[32] The membership of the corporation seems to have varied in number from twelve to twenty-four.

The school offered six departments, namely:

1. The Academic, embracing a four year course. This was designed to prepare the student for entering College or University and to provide the opportunity of acquiring a more general education and broader culture than is offered in the grade schools. Graduates were admitted to our church colleges and to the University of Minnesota without entrance examinations.

2. The Normal department, preparing young men and wom-

en for teaching public or parochial schools, arranged to meet the requirements of the State for the second grade teacher's certificate.

3. The Preparatory department, intended to serve the interests of those whose early education had been neglected or who for any reason were deficient in the common branches and could not be admitted into the Academic department.

4. The School of Commerce in which the purpose is not merely to fit students to become bookkeepers and other office help, but rather to train them that they may become men and women of ability and leaders in the community in which they live, trained so that the amanuensis desk shall only be a stepping stone to their life work.

5. The School of Music, which aims to develop capable and earnest musicians and also to afford opportunity for the study of music as part of a liberal education.

6. The School of Art. Instruction offered in drawing, the various branches of painting and pyrography.[33]

"In general," declares the College Quarterly, "our higher institutions of learning ought to promote the Kingdom of God, by creating desire among the young to serve the Lord and to develop their talents so that their services may bring the best possible results."[34] Therefore the Christianity courses held a very prominent place in the curriculum and the purpose of these was to "impart to the student a thorough and systematic knowledge of our faith and to furnish the most important factor in the development of his character."[35]

The rules which governed the students were very few since the youth were expected to "conduct themselves as Christian young ladies and gentlemen at all times." They were expected to attend chapel exercises each morning and divine services on Sundays. No use of tobacco in or about the buildings was allowed. Card playing, dancing, visiting saloons or billiard halls, indulging in intoxicating liquor, gambling, attending degrading theatrical performances, were strictly forbidden. These rules also applied to students living off the campus.[36] Students were not allowed to room "at other places in the city" as long as there was room available at the school; and when they were to live off the campus written requests were to be made. The College would furnish the students with an "approved list" of recommended homes.[37]

The library was enlarged year by year. Mr. Lin Lindquist, a member of the Corporation, promised a collection of about 5,000 labelled specimens of mineral ores, valued at $5,000 and equalling any collection of its kind in the State.[38]

There were a number of student organizations. The Aurora, organized in 1901, had as its aim the improvement in "oratory, discussion, parliamentary practice, singing and other exercises suited to the development of a harmonious and true Christian character." [39] It met Saturday evenings. The Atlanta for the young ladies met once a week for "instruction in fancy work and art needle work." This society was especially "beneficial to girls, because they have a chance to do this kind of work and at the same time receive a greater taste for charity work." [40] The Chorus was organized in 1901, the Band in 1902, the Athletic Association in 1904, the Tegnerförbundet and Mission Study Class in 1912. Then there were the Gladstone debating society, the College Orchestra, Glee Club and the Handel Oratorio Society which numbered up to ninety-five members. There were also other extracurricular activities.

Beginning January 1, 1905, the College catalogue was combined with the Quarterly which contained items of general interest. The subscription price was twenty-five cents a year.

Through the "Föreningen för Svenskhetens bevarande i Amerika (The Society for the Preservation of the Swedish in America) the school received (in 1912) a stipend of $15 for the student highest in rank in the Swedish language and literature.

J. H. Randahl
1850-1924

J. O. Cavallin
1844-1926

L. P. Lundgren
1851-1926

L. P. Stenstrom
1843-1926

Courtesy Minn. Conf.
Olof Fahlin

The donor was N. A. Nelson of Scandia Life (Mutual Trust) Insurance Company.[41] There was also an "Old Settlers Endowment Fund" for a chair in Christianity and Swedish. Some of the early pioneers gave $100 each for this fund. It also received a royalty from the sale of Kronberg's book, "Banbrytaren."

The commencements were especially festive occasions. Not only were the programs well planned and well rendered, but the attendance was good. The pastors of the District were there almost to a man and they usually stayed all day. Many were also in attendance from the congregations.

Necessary expenses included: matriculation fee $2.00, tuition—thirty weeks $30.00, one term of 12 weeks $12.00; School of Commerce—entire year $45.00, one term of 12 weeks $17.00; Bookkeeping $10.00. The first catalogue presents an interesting illustration of estimate of cost for the winter term: board and room, $27.60; tuition, matriculation and book rent $12.00; railroad fare, $2.42; clothing and laundry $2.00; subscriptions $1.50; incidentals, stationery, etc., $3.50—total $49.02. If a student worked for his board and roomed at the College the estimated expenses were brought to $26.65. In 1911 this sum had risen to $175.[42]

The position of Principal was held by the following: Anton Youngdahl, 1901-1910; James Moody, 1910-1911; E. Goranson, 1911-1913; F. A. Linder, 1913-1914; James Moody, 1914-1915; Carl Solomonson, 1915-1918; N. P. Langsjoen, 1918-1932.

The history of Northwestern College is very much like a summer day. It has a beautiful sunrise. During the hours of the day there are moments when the sun shines bright, only to be followed by moments when the sun goes behind the clouds. In the sixth year of its existence the president of the school states optimistically that "it has probably overcome the greatest hindrances, though the struggle for survival may yet continue." [43] A bright ray of sunlight shone through when the president could report that "four of our former students have enrolled in the Augustana Seminary and four others are ready to apply." [44] Or when money was gathered for the payment of an indebtedness of $21,500. The members of the Corporation subscribed about one-fourth of this sum and Mr. J. J. Hill gave $2,500. [45] Yet even standing in this high spot the president sees clouds on the horizon. Rejoicing that the debt was paid, the problem still remained: "How to cover the expenses and to keep up the standards with the little income received." [46]

While Northwestern College was busy in the sphere of its calling the sand in the hourglass was running low. It became evident that the institution could not continue as it was and therefore began to make special appeals to the Conference for help. [47]

But we shall stop at this point and turn our attention to a sister institution.

North Star College, 1908-1936

"The Red River Valley is not confined to raising cereals. Of late years great strides have been made in diversified farming and today the farmer is not only prepared to furnish the bread, but also the butter to spread on it, and also the beef, pork and mutton that go to make up a substantial meal"—so writes the Warren Sheaf, September 12, 1907. And in the realm of the church the interests and activities were also becoming enlarged.

In the early eighties Mr. J. P. Mattson conducted classes in Warren, Minnesota, in academic subjects. "That work inspired others and soon there were several from this part of the State who found their way to other denominational schools." [48]

About a quarter of a century later at a meeting of the Red River District (January 29, 1908) it was resolved, "that the Red River District recommends that a denominational school be established in Warren." A month later a meeting was held of interested pastors and laymen. The Articles of Incorporation were signed in the city of Warren, February 14, 1908, and the purpose stated as that of establishing "a denominational school." The incorporators were: Pastor E. O. Chelgren, John P. Mattson, John Lindberg, Aug. Lundgren, P. B. Mahlberg, Aaron Johnson, Nels Johnson, L. M. Olson, Nels Bystrom, C. H. Lindberg, John Westman, John W. Johnson, Alfred Johnson, Peter Dahlquist, Evart Dagoberg, John P. Dahlquist and Erick Olson. The name of the school was to be "The North Star College" and it was to be owned and controlled by members of the Swedish Lutheran Augustana Synod, but the school facilities were to be open to students of all denominations. "Hence it will fill a long felt need in this part of the Northwest from which it will draw its students." [49]

The first officers were: Pastor E. O. Chelgren, president; Aug. Lundgren, vice president; John Mattson, secretary; L. M. Olson, treasurer. The officers together with John Lindberg, Alfred Johnson, P. B. Mahlberg were the first Board of Trustees. [50]

The stated purpose of the school was to give a thorough training in the various branches of study, which are necessary as foundation for more advanced education. The instruction was to be based on sound Christian principles, "strengthened both by precept and by example. It shall serve primarily the interests of the Lutheran Church." [51]

Preparations were made immediately for the opening of the school. Prof. O. E. Abrahamson, teacher of English and Biology at Red Wing Academy was called to the principalship. He did not only come "highly recommended as a scholar and teacher," [52] but he helped to arrange for the opening of the school. The local press reported that he "will devote his time largely to advertise the new institution and solicit students." He brought with him a motorcycle, which "he will use in traveling about the country. Wherever he is seen moving along at a rapid rate of speed, let no one get scared, but halt him and

99

walk right up to him and let him do you good." [53] Prof. C. E.
Sjostrand of Lake City, Minnesota, accepted the call to be
Principal of the Commercial department. "He is a successful
and competent teacher of many years experience in that line
of work, having taught bookkeeping, stenography and penmanship at Luther College, Wahoo, Nebraska, for a number
of years." [54] The Warren Business College which had operated for a number of years was absorbed by North Star College.

The Warren Sheaf of September 24, 1908, carried this an-
nouncement:

NORTH STAR COLLEGE

School begins October 1, 1908, with instruction in the
following:

Academic	Shorthand
Preparatory	A course in Agriculture
Music	
Commercial	For information, phone or write
Telegraphic	O. E. Abrahamson
Typewriting	Principal.

At North Star College the instruction is the very best.
The rates are low and from the various departments you
can choose a course to suit yourself. Why travel hundreds
of miles to school when you have the best at home? When
considering schools remember North Star College.

In the same issue of the paper the information is furnished
that "we will have Saturday for our regular (class) work.
There will then be no occasion to study on Sunday."

The North Star Benefit Association with headquarters in
Moline, Ill., organized and established an Observatory at North
Star College in October, 1908, known as "Observatory 74,"
with about twenty charter members of prominent business
men of the city." [55]

In March 1909 a Domestic Science course was added to the curriculum,[56] and the next year a Correspondence department was added.[57]

Special emphasis was placed on the possibility for students to cover the four years Academy work in three years. The reason given for this—"the students are older and therefore realize the value of time and labor, they have a strong desire to seek knowledge and they spend all their time on the school-work."[58]

The first graduation was held May 2, 1909, "bringing to an auspicious close the first year of this promising institution of learning." [59] Hon. G. H. Mattson, Roseau, Representative in the State Legislature, delivered an address on the "Brotherhood of Man."

The school was first housed in the upper story of the Washington School building and in an adjoining family home, where the music department carried on its work. A portion of Prof. Abrahamson's home was also used. For a year and a half the old opera house, having been partitioned off for classrooms, housed the entire school. Some of the problems encountered may be surmised from such notices as, "in a few days someone from the College will canvass the city for places where students may room and board. We hope to start a boarding club, yet many want to board where they have their rooms." [60] About the same time, however, it was reported that "we have splendid accommodations for a large number of students. Classrooms are large and well ventilated, steamheated, finished in hardwood." [61]

In March 1910 the Board decided to erect a suitable building, costing in the neighborhood of $30,000. Pastor G. Wahlund was engaged as solicitor of funds. "This young institution has had a phenomenal growth—the attendance during this second year numbers more than a hundred." [62] Pastor Wahlund became Field Secretary and General Manager.

The cornerstone for the new building was laid October 16, 1911, with "impressive and imposing public ceremonies." The mayor of the city proclaimed a public holiday and business houses were closed during the ceremony. Public school ceased for the day. Dr. Gustav Andreen, President of Augustana College, Rock Island, Ill., "attired in his full costume indicative of scholarship, the cap and gown of a Doctor's degree," was the speaker. His text was 2 Kings 6:1-7, and he concluded: "Let this building be erected to the glory and honor of God and the general good of humanity and may it stand as a monument of devotion of its founders and friends." [63]

Nearly a month later, November 11, 1913, the building was dedicated with the governor of the State, Eberhardt, as speaker. $3,830 was subscribed at the dedication services, which indicated the fervor and enthusiasm of the supporters of the institution.

The building, of distinctly College type and Swedish architecture, was ninety feet long and seventy feet wide, four stories high. It had three entrances. The basement contained the gymnasium, lavatories, store rooms, matron's quarters, kitchen and dining hall. On the first floor were classrooms, chapel, office rooms, music rooms, cloak rooms and library. On the second floor were rooms for the Commercial department, recitation rooms, cloak rooms and museum. The third floor was planned for dormitory rooms. The cost of the building was $65,000. The school moved into this new home in 1913. At the time of the erection there was a large debt on the building, but in three years this was paid through the generosity of the people in and around Warren and through the magnificent gift of $9,000 by Hon. J. J. Hill. In 1921 a four hundred and eighty acre farm, valued at forty dollars an acre, became the property of the College through the courtesy of a Warren man.[64]

During Mr. Sjostrand's incumbency the third story of the College building was remodelled so as to make adequate rooms for the lady students enrolled. Through the generosity of congregations, Ladies' Aids, Luther Leagues, etc., this was completed without any indebtedness being incurred. Many pastors and members of the congregations in the Red River District came to assist in this work. Thus the lathing was done largely by women. Mr. Sjostrand drove from congregation to congregation presenting this particular project and gathered money sufficient to pay for this major improvement. Approximately thirty women were housed in very comfortable rooms.

When the school opened there were eight students enrolled and at the close of the first year the attendance was 56. In 1911-1912 the enrollment was 208 in all departments; in 1920 it was 232, in 1921 it reached 253. From the latter year, due to the economic conditions and other causes, the attendance began to wane. A number of graduates continued through College and Seminary into the holy ministry. Many others in various walks of life received guidance and help through North Star College.

The Museum had a fine collection of forty mounted mammals, ninety mounted birds, fish, reptiles, besides Indian curios and relics.

The following served as presidents of North Star College: Prof. O. E. Abrahamson, 1908-1915; Prof. C. E. Sjostrand, 1915-1923; Pastor Albin A. Larson, 1923-1936.

In the Struggle for Survival

Already in 1914 the president of Northwestern College declared in his report: "Our schools must often struggle desperately to survive, but in spite of the obstacles in the way, we

must trust God and say with David, 'I shall not die, but live.' "[65]
And this could be applied to both schools. They did struggle
on tenaciously, courageously and hopefully. There were also
encouragements. Through the school paper, "Kyrka och
Skola" (Church and School), from Northwestern College and
"The North Star Signal" from North Star, the cause of Christian education was presented to the people. But the Red River
Valley Conference school carts began to ride heavily and the
way seemed to become constantly worse.

In 1917 a resolution was presented to the Conference from
both the Corporations expressing the confidence that the
work of the schools could more conveniently and efficiently
be carried on by the Conference as such. The Corporations
were asked to submit the conditions on which they would be
willing to surrender their respective institutions and a committee was elected to confer with the Corporations in this matter.
The following year this committee reported that it had surveyed both institutions and it recommended:

1. That we do not think the Conference is able to support two
   schools within its territory.

2. That the Conference can not take over any of the schools,
   except on condition, that it may have full freedom in the
   disposition of the properties.

3. In case the Corporations are not willing to turn over the
   institutions on the above conditions, the Conference is not
   obliged to ask the congregations to assume financial obligations for their support.

The Conference decided, that the second point be adopted
and the other two be deleted.[66]

Two years later both institutions were offered to the congregations unconditionally,[67] and the matter was submitted to
the congregations for a referendum, but they replied with a
negative vote.[68] The Mission Board presented a resolution

acknowledging the work performed by the schools and expressing the confidence that the people will continue to support them.

In 1925 the Conference president reported that both schools had had trying years because of decreased attendance [69] and the following year he stated, that the "pastors consider it wise that there be but one school." [70] One pastor had reported: "If we could unite the schools into one, all would be well. But now says Samaria: 'Our fathers have worshiped in this mountain.' And Jerusalem says: 'Jerusalem is the place to worship.' Well, there you are. Sometimes I think: 'The time will come when neither in this mountain nor in Jerusalem.' " [71]

The Mission Board was authorized to suggest how the school question might be solved. The Board asked the school Corporations if they were willing to surrender their institutions to the Conference in order that they might be merged into one. North Star said "No" to this proposal and Northwestern declared it was willing on the condition: 1. That both schools be submitted unconditionally; 2 that in case N.S.C. is not willing to surrender, Northwestern College be the future seat for the educational work in the Conference. The Mission Board recommended the second proposal which was also adopted by a vote of fifty-seven to thirty-two. The matter was again submitted to the congregations. The referendum vote was forty in favor and forty-nine against. Five congregations did not vote.

In 1930 the school question was again thoroughly discussed. The Conference expressed its gratitude to the teachers of both institutions and to the people who had supported the work. It was also decided, that financial aid be given only one of our Church schools; that this be given to Northwestern College; that part of the school appropriation be placed in an emergency fund under the jurisdiction of the Mission Board, to be used in case North Star College ceases to operate or is in danger of losing its property; that [72] the Mission Board ascertain if the Corporations are willing to turn over their properties unconditionally. North Star refused to surrender to the referendum. In 1932 the Northwestern College Corporation offered its institution with assets and liabilities to the Conference—since the Articles of Incorporation prescribe that in case of dissolution of the Corporation the net assets shall go to the Red River Valley Conference.[73] Says the president of the Conference: "We regret that this school, which has served us so faithfully thirty-two years, is now questioning whether it shall continue or not." [74] The president of the school reports to the same meeting: "The authorities of the school have thus formulated no plans for the next year's work. In a summary it can and must be said: The Academy by itself can scarcely be kept up during the present hard times. Full Junior college work, which would meet the demands of our people and justify the continuance of the work, is too expensive for our College Corporation." The Northwestern College Corporation offered this resolution:

"Whereas Northwestern College Corporation is finding it exceedingly difficult to continue school work due primarily to the shortage of students and lack of financial support;[75]

"Whereas the Constitution of this Corporation prescribes, that in case of dissolution its net corporate assets be turned over to the Red River Conference of the Evangelical Lutheran Augustana Synod,

Therefore resolved that we now offer the Northwestern College with its assets and liabilities to said Conference, and if said Conference accepts this offer, the Board of Directors of this Corporation be and are hereby authorized and instructed to convey the property to said Conference."

The Conference resolved to accept the offer as submitted and authorized the Mission Board to accept the property on behalf of the Conference, with authority to "hold, rent or sell the property in whole or in part, as well as taking care of the encumbrances." [76]

Thus another warrior for the Lord went down to defeat due to the changed conditions, with high schools in every town, the war situation and economic distress. Northwestern had fought a good fight for a little more than thirty-two years. This weak and bleeding warrior was received into the hands of the Conference Executive Committee June 22, 1932. The equally brave wrestler for the Lord to the North, continued a little longer, but weakened until it, too, succumbed. As a derelict vessel they foundered among the rocks of modern changed conditions. The curtain falls on the stage of the schools of the Red River Valley Conference. The final sentence in the last report of the president of Northwestern College to the Conference can be applied to this entire chapter:

"Speaking of thankfulness we are most of all grateful to God for permitting us for a season to take part in His work." [77]

References

[1] Anderson, Mrs. Chas. L. History of Bethesda Church, Moorhead, Minn., for Seventieth Anniversary, April 29, 1950 MSS.
[2] Catalogue, Hope Academy, 1889-1890, p. 18. A quite complete set of Catalogues from the Hope Academy is found in the Archives at Augustana College, Rock Island, Ill.
[3] Skaffaren, February 28, 1894.
[4] Catalogue, Hope Academy, 1889-1890, p. 19.
[5] Skaffaren, May 21, 1890. "W" in "Omnibus."
[6] Ibid, August 20, 1890.
[7] Ibid, August 20, 1890.
[8] Catalogue, Hope Academy, 1892-93, p. 13.
[9] Ibid, 1890-91, p. 21.
[10] Ibid, 1893-94, p. 6.
[11] Ibid, 1892-93, p. 12.
[12] Skaffaren, August 20, 1890. "Hallock News."
[13] Skaffaren, August 27, 1890.
The Hope Academy Catalogue, 1889-90, has the following personnel listed: Officers of the Lutheran Benevolent Society of the Red River Valley—President, J. O. Cavallin; Vice President, J. Moody; Secretary, J. P. Mattson; Treasurer, E. Bjorkquist.

Board of Directors—Mr. J. L. Bjorkquist, President, Moorhead, Minn.; Mr. Louis Johnson, Secretary; Mr. S. E. Eastlund, Solicitor, Moorhead, Minn.; Mr. F. Boman, Sheyenne, N. Dak.; Pastor S. A. Lindholm, Lake Park, Minn.; Mr. Peter Dahlquist, Warren, Minn.; Pastor S. G. Swenson, Hallock, Minn. Faculty—Rev. J. O. Cavallin, Principal, Religious Instruction; S. A. Challman, Assistant Principal, English Language and Latin; J. P. Mattson, Secretary, History, Geography and Pedagogy; Lena Brown, Instrumental Music and Domestic Art; Rev. S. Udden, Swedish Language and Vocal Music; Grace McMillan, Librarian, Mathematics, Bookkeeping and Penmanship; Assistant Librarians—Mary Nelson, Anna Wedin, Herman Lundquist, Elof Peterson. Other teachers—Joseph Anderson, A.B.; H. W. Ryding, who also was Principal, 1893-4; L. W. Kling, Minnie Eastlund, J. R. Brown, B.Sc.; Christine Larson, Mrs. S. A. Challman, M.Accts.; N. Keyland, A.M.

Writes Dr. A. Bergin: "Small in stature and thin are the teachers, most of them; but nevertheless they do good work and are loved and admired by the students." (Skaffaren, April 17, 1895.)

14 Catalogue, Hope Academy, 1882-83, p. 14.
15 Ibid, p. 15.
16 Anderson, Mrs. Chas. L. History of Bethesda Church, Moorhead, Minn. MSS. "Miss Dahlquist will accompany the youthful singing-group from Hope Academy which now has started its tour representing the school." (Minnesota Stats Tidning, May 27, 1896.)
17 Skaffaren, May 28,1890.
18 Skaffaren, November 7, 1894.
19 Ibid, September 26, 1895.
20 Ibid, December 11, 1895.
21 Kronberg, S. J. Banbrytaren, p. 397.
22 Ibid, p. 398.
23 Minutes, Minnesota Conference, 1900, p. 12, 18.
24 Lindholm, S. A. Minnesota Stats Tidning, February 15, 1905.
25 Minutes, Alexandria District, April 6, 1899.
26 Minnesskrift, Minnesota Konferensens Femtio-ars Jubileum, p. 238.
27 Catalogue, 1901, p. 6. A few Catalogues from Northwestern College are found in the R.R.V. Conference vault at Bethany Home, Alexandria, Minn.
28 Prairieblomman, 1909, p. 190.
29 Catalogue, 1911, p. 9.
30 Kronberg, S. J. Banbrytaren, p. 400. Prairieblomman, 1909.
31 Prairieblomman, 1909, p. 190.
32 Catalogue, 1903. p. 5.
33 Ibid, 1912, pp. 15, 23, 25, 26, 32, 41.
34 N.W.C. Quarterly, 1908, p. 10.
35 Catalogue, 1903, p. 12.
36 Ibid, 1903, p. 31.
37 Ibid, 1903, p. 31; 1904, p. 36.
38 Ibid, 1903, p. 34.
39 Ibid, 1902, p. 21.
40 Ibid, 1909, p. 12.
41 Ibid, 1911-12, p. 14.
42 Ibid, 1911, p. 42.

Among the instructors—besides the Principals—may be mentioned: Eric Floren, A. C. Holmquist, Tobias Tjornholm, Lillian Rosberg, Beda Murk, Catherine Goetzinger, Albert Hegstrom, Clara M. Hoorn, Selma Malmgren, J. Gustave Lundholm, Eva M. Hasselquist, E. Louise Aldrich, L. E. Kleppe, John Olson, F. A. Linder, Alma Videen, Leonard Lake, A. L. Berglund, Emelia Hoorn, M. N. Lundquist, Fanny Bernser, Eva C. Noelch, Frans Sucker, Alice Peterson, Axel Anderson, Ella Mork, Dagmar Peterson, Luther Hanson, H. T. Yngve, N. T. Anderson, Edythe L. E. Johnson, Olive B. Pearson, Inez Field, Oscar Backstrom, Reuben Kron, Minnie Benson, Jacob Langsjoen, Carrie Hawkinson, Ebba Leaf, Arthur Pikop, Marvin Larson, Esther Peterson, Victor E. Matson, Viola Olin, Verner Matson, Anna Larson, Hazel von Arnan Christenson, Clarence P. Hall, Dorothy Hall, Helen Ording, Vivian Sand, Ruth G. Peterson.

43 Minutes, Minnesota Conference, 1906, 1907, p. 40, 41.
44 Minutes, R.R.V. Conference, 1913, p. 53.
45 Ibid, 1916, p. 35, 36.
46 Ibid, 1916, p. 37.
47 Ibid, 1917, p. 41-42.
48 Circular to Congregation of the R.R.V. Conference.
49 Warren Sheaf, February 20, 1908.
50 Ibid, February 20, 1908.
51 Circular to Congregations R.R.V. Conference.
52 Warren Sheaf, May 14, 1908.
53 Ibid, August 6, 1908.
54 Ibid, May 28, 1908.
55 Ibid, October 8, 1908.
56 Ibid, March 11, 1908.
57 Ibid, November 17, 1916.
58 Ibid, August 25, 1910.
59 Ibid, May 27, 1909.
60 Ibid, September 9, 1909.

[61] Ibid, October 28, 1909.
[62] Ibid, March 10, 1910.
[63] Ibid, October 19, 1911.
[64] Circular to Congregations of the R.R.V. Conference.
[65] Minutes, R.R.V. Conference, 1914, p. 39.
[66] Ibid, 1918, p. 49.
[67] Ibid, 1931, p. 19.
[68] Ibid, 1922, p. 54.
[69] Ibid, 1925, p. 28.
[70] Ibid, 1926, p. 19.
[71] Ibid, 1926, p. 19.
[72] Ibid, 1930, p. 56.
[73] Ibid, 1932, p. 20.
[74] Ibid, 1932, p. 20.
[75] Ibid, 1932, p. 46.
[76] Ibid, 1932, p. 46.
[77] Ibid, 1932, p. 44.
We have not been able to locate any Catalogues from North Star College.

VII. CHARITY

Warren Hospital

At the first annual meeting of the Red River Valley Conference, held in Warren, Minnesota, March 12-16, 1913, the Warren Hospital, valued at $36,000, was offered to the Conference on condition that it be continued as a hospital. Further it was stipulated that any profit which may occur be used for improvements on the institution; and that in case it would revert back to the Corporation it would be in the same condition as when it was taken over. A committee of one pastor and one layman from each District was elected to visit the institution, confer with the hospital Corporation and then report. Members of the Committee were: Pastors J. Moody, F. N. Anderson, N. Lehart; Laymen C. H. Larson, Aug. Clauson, C. J. Carlson. The report of the committee was favorable and the following resolution was adopted: "That the Conference requests the Red River District to effect an incorporated organization which may receive the hospital as a gift; and that the Conference pledges an annual offering for the free-patient fund of the hospital." [1]

The following year it was reported that the Corporation had been formed and the documents were ready. It was therefore resolved, "That the Conference gratefully receives the Warren Hospital as a gift and that—in accordance with the Constitution, Chapter I, Article 3, paragraph 2—the matter be referred to the congregations for a referendum vote." [2] The transfer had not been effected by the next annual meeting and resolutions were accordingly repeated.[3] The referendum vote did not carry, but the printed minutes do not report the actual result and remain silent on the whole question until 1920 when

110

the president urges that the hospital work be put on the program of the Conference.[4] By resolution the Board of Charities is instructed to make investigations and preparations for such work; also that in case the Board receives a favorable offer the congregations be informed.[5]

The president of the Conference reports in his annual message in 1921: "Last summer the Warren Hospital, Warren, Minnesota, was offered as a gift to the Conference. The institution is valued at $100,000. The Board of Charities presented the matter—according to the Conference constitution and resolution—to the congregations for a referendum. Fifty-nine congregations voted in the affirmative. By this vote our people have declared that they will enter into the eleemosynary work among the sick and needy. The Deed has been executed and completed. Through this institution our church will carry on a glorious God-pleasing mission." [6]

The Conference resolved, that
"Inasmuch as the Board of Charities has acted in accordance with the resolutions of the Conference, in its resolutions of 1920, and has in accordance with said decision taken over the Warren Hospital, valued at about $100,000, therefore resolved that the Conference empowers the Board of Charities to direct the work at the hospital in accordance with its constitution." [7]

A brief resume of the circular sent the congregations gives us an idea of the institution as such. The hospital was built in 1907 with a bed capacity of forty which in 1920 was increased to fifty-five. A two-year training school for nurses was maintained. The staff consisted of five doctors. From the beginning the hospital had payed for itself. Because of extensive improvements and repairs there was an indebtedness of $12,000.

The conditions on which the hospital was turned over to the church were (in part):
1. That the Church assumes all indebtedness.

2. That the institution continues to maintain an efficient training school for nurses.

3. That the hospital be open to all reputable physicians, but that no doctor may practice in the institution or do any surgery except that his qualifications be first passed upon by a member of the American College of Surgeons.

4. That the firm of Drs. Bratrud and Meland shall continue to have the privilege of office space in the building, that additional room be granted them as required and that this shall continue for a period of five years.

5. That the hospital be conducted and operated along the lines laid down by the American College of Surgeons and that the Association will see to it that all records are kept up to date for this standardization.

6. That the hospital board be made up in such a way, that there be at least one local member from Warren to see that local needs are safeguarded.

A communication from the Warren Hospital Association was also submitted to the Conference:

"To the Red River Valley Conference of the Augustana Synod.

"Gentlemen:

"In transmitting to you the title papers of the Warren Hospital Association it was thought appropriate to inform you that at a meeting held at the City Hall in Warren, on May 6, 1921, the following resolution was unanimously adopted by the officers and members of the Warren Hospital Association:

"Inasmuch as the property of the Warren Hospital Association has now been appropriately transferred to the Red River Valley Conference of the Augustana Synod, and

"Inasmuch as the members of the Warren Hospital Association feel that the transfer of the property is to the best interest of the people whom the Association served, and

Bethany Home for the Aged
Alexandria, Minnesota

Warren Hospital
Warren, Minnesota

"Inasmuch as the Red River Valley Conference is about to take up the work heretofore done by the Warren Hospital Association, and

"Inasmuch as the work and service to be done and performed hereafter will greatly exceed the work and service heretofore done by the Association,

"Therefore be it resolved,

"That the officers and members of the Warren Hospital Association send greetings and good wishes to the officers and members of the Red River Valley Conference of the Augustana Synod; that we express unto them our utmost good wishes and hope that the work and service of the hospital may be greatly increased and improved; that the burdens heretofore resting upon the shoulders of an organization that started some fifteen years ago under adverse circumstances, with no capital, no prestige and with considerable opposition, both latent and apparent, are now happily overcome and the hospital made into an institution of great prospect of increased service and efficiency.

"The members of the old organization feel that they have performed good service and now gladly surrender (to) the new organization the entire property that has accumulated, doing so in the hope and with the expectation that the new organization can and will better perform the service heretofore done by the old.

"May the Warren Hospital forever live as an institution of service to all the people without favoritism to any class or creed, having as its object the relief of the sick, the infirm and the crippled, constantly extending a helping hand to all such as be worthy.

"Very respectfully,

"Warren Hospital Association,

"By C. E. Lundquist, President.

"Att.: L. M. Olson, Secretary."

The president of the Conference was instructed to officially thank the Warren Hospital Association for the donation of the hospital, and a committee was also elected to present suitable resolutions. This report was as follows:

"To the Officers and Members of the Warren Hospital Association, Warren, Minnesota.

"Gentlemen:

"The Red River Valley Conference of the Augustana Synod, in meeting assembled, having received the kind and cordial greeting of good will and good wishes of the Warren Hospital Association, desires to express in return the sincerest gratitude and appreciation of said greeting. We as a Conference hereby desire to voice our profound appreciation of the labor done by the Warren Hospital Association in a work commenced under adverse circumstances, continued under difficulties, and brought to a successful state of efficiency through perseverance, faith and willingness to sacrifice for a worthy cause. We highly honor the spirit which decided to surrender an institution brought up to the full measure of success, because of an unselfish belief that under a different authority and auspices an eminently worthy work might be made still more worthy and useful. We greatly esteem and value the confidence placed in us by the gentlemen of the Warren Hospital Association to continue the work thus entrusted to us, to perform it in conformity with the conditions outlined, to pursue the aim and purpose of the original founders of the Hospital, to endeavor to maintain the prestige which the institution under the former management has won and so richly deserved, and with the help of God hope to further widen this aim and purpose and heighten this prestige.

"In this work, we hope to be favored with your further confidence, the counsel of your experience, and your continued co-operative sympathy. As a religious organization we are deeply conscious of the great opportunities for the work of blessed charity which your magnanimity has bestowed upon us; and as we hope for God's aid and blessing upon the work to be now undertaken by us, we hope and pray for God's richest blessings upon you for the work you have done, for the spirit you have shown, and the interest and good will which we hope will always be from you to us.

"By order of the Red River Valley Conference.

"K. Rosenthal, N. P. Langsjoen, C. G. Zaar, Committee."[8]

The Hospital has carried on its important work and has also directly and indirectly served the Church. At first there were over a thousand patients a year. Thus a Conference president states in his message: "Ten years ago there were very few hospitals and far between in this neighborhood. Now nearly all doctors have a small so-called hospital where they may bring their patients."[9] That trials, problems and difficulties arise is but natural. The hospital is an "abode of sorrow and joy."[10] The doctors connected with this hospital when it was turned over to the Conference, severed their connection with it. Naturally this was a hard blow. The School of Nursing was also closed for a few years. But we also read: "Since the Board of Charities took over the institution it has made marked progress."[11] The hospital has not only rendered proficient service, but it has done much charity work and there has been a Christian atmosphere prevailing. Morning devotions are conducted every day. Christianity courses constitute a regular part of the nurses training curriculum. A Missionary Society has rendered valuable services. Reports a hospital chaplain: "Often we find a poor sinner on the bed of suffering confessing his Savior and believing the forgiveness of sin."[12]

The Hospital is on the approved list of the American College of Surgeons.

The Bethany Home for the Aged

At the very first annual convention of the Red River Valley Conference it was resolved, "That a committee of three be elected to make preliminary investigations as to a suitable place and best offers for the location of an orphanage and home for the aged within the Conference and report at the next meeting." [13]

Members of the committee were: Aug. Lundgren, Pastors H. S. Chilgren and S. W. Swenson. Two years later the committee reported that it had approached the cities of Detroit Lakes, Lake Park and Alexandria, the last named offering the best inducement—six acres of land beautifully located near a lake six blocks from the Svea Lutheran church; with the option of buying more land at a reasonable price; and also a $1,500 cash donation, providing the institution be located there and that a permanent building be erected at a cost of not less than $15,000.[14] The land was donated by Mr. Christ Raiter.[15]

The Conference accepted the offer and the matter was referred to the congregations for a referendum. A Board of Charities of nine members was also elected. This Board was instructed to submit to the Conference a constitution for the work in general and for the Home for the Aged in particular. Furthermore the Board was to present at the next annual Conference meeting plans and specifications for a building. Members of the first Board were: Pastors S. W. Swenson, P. E. Ording, F. M. Eckman, L. P. Lundgren and Messrs. C. H. Larson, J. A. Wallin, Nils Heigg, O. A. Naplin and Aug. Lundgren.

The result of the referendum was, that out of ninety-one congregations in the Conference sixty-two voted in favor, fourteen voted in the negative and fifteen did not express themselves.[16] At the meeting of the Conference, 1916, a "temporary" Board of Charities submitted a proposed constitution. The Conference adopted it and decided that the Board shall be incorporated if it finds this to be advisable; that it be authorized to go ahead with the erection of a building which shall not exceed in cost $25,000—without the furniture. The building committee had as members, Pastors F. M. Eckman, B. Modin and Mr. C. H. Larson. Pastors S. W. Swenson, P. E. Ording and Mr. Aug. Lundgren were a committee to secure sketches for the building.

The first report from the Board to the Conference was presented at the meeting in Fergus Falls, Minnesota, March 1916. The president of the Board, Dr. S. W. Swenson, reported that the instructions from the Conference had been carried out; the building contract had been submitted to the bidders and the Hansen and Pinnar firm were the lowest bidders—$19,997.00. The size of the building was ninety by thirty-eight feet, four stories high including basement. The material was pressed brick. The building was to be completely modern. The cornerstone was laid September 4, 1916, and the building dedicated July 3, 1917. The Home received its first guests on New Year's Day, 1917. The first report mentions that ten rooms had been furnished by individuals, churches and organizations at a cost of $75.00 a room.[17]

The Conference expressed its satisfaction over the results of the efforts by the Board of Charities and authorized the appointment of a superintendent when deemed necessary. The next year the Board reported that there were twenty-four persons receiving "four square meals" daily. A barn had been built and trees planted. The Conference was filled with joy and satisfaction at the accomplishments and urged the congregations to lift offerings during the month of November for the "Charity Fund" at the Home. The need of this Fund is evident when we read in 1932 that seventeen persons were charity guests—"free boarders"—at the Home.[18]

Already in 1919 mention is made of the need of enlarged facilities, but because of the depression times nothing was done beyond discussing the matter.[19]

In 1922 the Board of Charities report contains two sections: A. Bethany Home, B. Warren Hospital. Plans were submitted for an addition to the Home and the following year the Board was authorized to go ahead with building plans. During the next year the annex building was erected at a cost of $30,000. It had thirty-two rooms, besides the assembly and furnace rooms. It was dedicated August 12, 1924. Since that time a "Donation Day" has been observed annually—now set for the first Thursday in October. The second year after its completion it was reported that "the Home is filled." [20]

Duties of the Superintendent of Bethany Home

1. The Superintendent shall be a person of Christian character and of proved ability, whose first and principal duty shall be to exemplify Christian principles in the management of the institution and in conduct generally.

2. The Superintendent shall be the official representative of the Board and its committees in the management of the institution and shall be responsible to the Board for his or her official acts. It shall be the Superintendent's duty to see to it, that the provisions of the constitution and the regulations prescribed by the Board are carried out and that persons employed at the institution perform their duties faithfully.

3. The Superintendent shall attend to the general correspondence of the institution and shall refer to the proper authorities all applications for admission to the Home and all other matters requiring action by the Board or any of its committees.

4. The Superintendent shall have charge of the devotional exercises morning and evening at the Home.

5. Subject to the rules and actions by the Board the Superintendent shall maintain the discipline and have power to engage or dismiss all servants in or about the institution unless otherwise specified by the Board.

6. The Superintendent shall attend to all ordinary purchases of supplies for the institution and make payments for the maintenance of the institution as the Board from time to time may designate.

7. The Superintendent shall keep on file a duplicate of all correspondence pertaining to the institution and perform such other duties as the Board may direct from time to time.[21]

On the 9th day of April, 1927, the one hundredth birthday anniversary of Kajsa Äng, one of the guests at the Home, was observed with great festivities.

At one of the Conference meetings the president of the Board complained that "the Board has been given power to build and manage, but no money has been provided." Much of the money received has been used for charity cases.[22] At the same meeting the Conference appropriated $4,500 for charity— the Warren Hospital receiving $2,000, Bethany Home $2,000 and the Children's Home $500. In 1932 there were forty-five persons at the Home under life contracts. The present policy of the Board is to discourage life contracts in place of monthly payments.

The condition of the times is mirrored in the Conference decision in 1932, that the appropriation be reduced to $3,500. In a report from the Board we read: "When you compare the maintenance cost of our institution with similar institutions in the Synod, you will find that your Board has been very careful all these years. No special ingathering, no financial drive of any kind has been undertaken. I do not think you find a similar case at any institution of our Synod."[23] However, six years later (1938) the Conference decided "that the Board be authorized to conduct an ingathering for $30,000 for the payment of the debt." A sum of $18,007.32 was received.

Mr. C. H. Larson was treasurer the first year and was succeeded by Pastor P. E. Ording who served until his death in 1937. Since then Mr. Emil E. Gahlon has filled this position.

Miss Mary Johnson, daughter of one of the pioneer pastors of the District, was the first matron. "She loves her work and performs it efficiently, not for wages, but in love and enthusiasm for the cause, offers her strength in the service of the Home and the Conference." [24] When she was compelled to resign because of ill health in 1919, she gave evidence of her abiding love for the institution in that she gave $200 to the Home for the Aged and $344.27 to the Children's Home. Miss Johnson was followed by Mrs. J. S. Ryding, who served two years. Sister Alma Olofson assumed charge November 15, 1921, and continued two and a half years. She was followed by Sister Albertina Gasman, who held the position from 1923 until the spring of 1930. In the latter year Sister Ingeborg Carlberg took up the work and continued with the institution until January 1, 1937. From that date Miss Ebba Anderson has been matron.

Pastor A. Mattson was chaplain at the Home until his death in 1932. Dr. O. O. Gustafson filled the position from 1932 until 1952.

A new chapter began in 1946 when the Conference resolved "That we sincerely call the attention of our people to the urgent need of extending the charity work in our Conference to include the proper care of the senile and invalids; that an ingathering of $100,000 be made during 1947; that the Executive Board of the Conference and the Board of Charities jointly prepare for and carry out this program; and that it be submitted to the free choice of our people to designate the institution for which their contribution is to be made." [25] Though the goal in this ingathering was not reached since about sixty-five per cent was received, yet the Conference erected in 1950-51 a most modern and convenient addition to the Home, so that the Bethany Home is equipped to care not only for the aged and infirm, but also for those who are invalids. The contract for the erection of the addition, including partial remodelling of the old building, was given to Mr. George Madsen of Minneapolis,

Minnesota. The cost of the construction and furnishing totalled $325,000. The cornerstone was laid April 22, 1951, and an impressive dedication service was held November 6, 1951, when the newly installed president of the Augustana Church, Dr. Oscar A. Benson, preached. The dedication service was held in connection with the annual Pastoral Conference in the Calvary Church, Alexandria.

During the thirty-five years this Home has been in operation a total of 486 persons have been admitted and cared for. Of these 293 have died here, 91 have left for one reason or another, and 102 are guests at present.

What a volume the life stories of these aged people would make, if they were open to our view and were recorded in their entirety. In many cases the day might have been stormy or at least operose and arduous. As the sand in the hourglass began to run low and the shadows began to fall, the horizon had glimmers of brightness and hope. There was a beautiful sunset at the end of life's way. The Red River Valley Conference had a share in providing the home and rest in the evening of life.

The Bethany Children's Home

At the very session at which the Board of Charities reported concerning the festive dedication of the first Home for the Aged, it was instructed to investigate the need and possibility of caring for orphan children. In anticipation of such activity the congregations were urged to gather money in the Sunday Schools for this branch of the charity program.[26]

The Board reported at the next annual Conference meeting that a survey had been made in the congregations to ascertain the need. Even though the response on the part of the pastors was very poor, the impression was received that the paramount need was for a receiving home. Accordingly the Board was instructed to investigate the laws concerning this type of work and report to the next annual meeting.[27] The Board was very prompt in complying with the wishes of the Conference, because at the next meeting it reported, that a house adjoining the Home for the Aged had been purchased at a price of $5,300. It was deemed advisable to secure this property in order that the Home for the Aged "may not get too close neighbors." The house could be used for a receiving home, if the Conference would so desire. At the same convention the Conference resolved, that "we express our satisfaction that the Board succeeded in acquiring a valuable property near Bethany Home for the Aged, so that ample room is now found for future needs." [28]

In his report to the Conference in 1922 the president of the Board says: "The Board is now ready to open a Receiving Home and welcomes therefore the defenseless little children to this our institution. We also hope that our people will support this work by liberal gifts and wills." [29] At this same time the ingathering in the Sunday Schools brought in $931.78. It is interesting to notice that 590 children solicited money through cards in the Sunday Schools for this work.[30] Certainly this was also a training for the children. "The children have been faithful and true friends for a number of years, and we are surely thankful to them for their love and willingness to solicit money for their little brothers and sisters at the orphanage." [31] By Conference resolution it was later (1931) decided that "we observe Children's Day and that St. Michael's Day be set aside as such and that pastors use that occasion to present to our people the privileges and responsibilities which we have in caring for the children at Bethany Home." [32]

In 1925 the president of the Board of Charities reports that "there seems to be no real need of work with the children in our Conference. We have no large cities and the few children in need can easily be cared for at the Lutheran Homes which already exist." [33] But the following year the same official reports that "we have during the year started a 'Receiving Home' work. Have already let out a small child for adoption in a devoutly Christian home. There are three children at the Home." [34]

In 1927 the Receiving Home activities are given their own heading and space in the Board of Charities report. It seems very appropriate when the president says: "This work is yet in its infancy in our Conference; but we have made a good start. It is a beautiful scene to watch the happy little ones." [35] The same report informs us that the work at the Children's Home was carried on in conjunction with the "Board of Christian Service" of the Minnesota Conference. This arrangement was made upon the advice of the State Board of Control. The work therefore took more the form of child placement—"to receive orphans and place them in respectable homes for adoption or ward." [36] One report explains very logically that most of the children come from broken homes; children that are either neglected or not wanted. "The fundamental idea is to find homes as near normal as possible for the children." [37]

In 1929 there were eleven children at the Home and "therefore there is a great need for enlarged facilities." There have been a number of misgivings about the work for the children; it has been suggested that it might be better to seek another location than near the Home for the Aged, that a more suitable Home should be erected if the work is to be continued. Therefore the Board has been asked to study the situation.[38]

In 1943 the status of the Bethany Children's Home was slightly changed in that the Board of Charities applied for a license to operate a Boarding Home for Children. This request was granted. At the same time the Child Welfare Work was continued in co-operation with the Board of Christian Service.[39]

Miss Amanda Larson, who had been assistant at the Home for the Aged, became matron at the Children's Home at the start and she served efficiently until she was compelled by reason of ill health to resign in 1942.[40] "Miss Amanda Larson is a kind and loving matron and the children find in her a sympathetic friend." [41] "She lived for the institution as if it were her own." [42] She was succeeded by Mrs. Alma Anderson, who in turn was followed by Mrs. Jean Larson in 1944. When she resigned, April 1, 1948, she was followed by Mrs. Clara Berg, who served until 1951 when Mrs. Kermit Rosenquist took charge.

References

[1] Minutes, R.R.V. Conference, 1913, p. 51-52.
[2] Ibid, 1914, p. 45.
[3] Ibid, 1915, p. 46-47.
[4] Ibid, 1920, p. 34.
[5] Ibid, 1921, p. 18.
[6] Ibid, 1921, p. 33.
[7] Ibid, 1921, p. 36-38.
[8] Ibid, 1921, p. 38.
[9] Ibid, 1929, p. 32.
[10] Ibid, 1931, p. 54.
[11] Ibid, 1931, p. 34.
[12] Ibid, 1923, p. 40.
[13] Ibid, 1913, p. 57.
[14] Ibid, 1915, p. 46.
[15] Ibid, 1931, p. 35.
[16] Ibid, 1916, p. 17.
[17] Ibid, 1917, p. 36.
[18] Ibid, 1918, p. 33.
[19] Ibid, 1920, p. 16.
[20] Ibid, 1922, p. 42.
[21] Ibid, 1920, p. 42.
[22] Ibid, 1928, p. 34.
[23] Ibid, 1933, p. 34.
[24] Ibid, 1917, p. 36.
[25] Ibid, 1946, p. 52.
[26] Ibid, 1918, p. 37.
[27] Ibid, 1919, p. 45, 46.
[28] Ibid, 1920, p. 34.
[29] Ibid, 1922, p. 32.
[30] Ibid, 1923, p. 50.
[31] Ibid, 1931, p. 33.
[32] Ibid, 1931, p. 40.
[33] Ibid, 1933, p. 33.
[34] Ibid, 1926, p. 32.
[35] Ibid, 1927, p. 30.
[36] Ibid, 1937, p. 37.
[37] Ibid, 1940, p. 43.
[38] Ibid, 1929, p. 31, 39; 1953, p. 11.
[39] Ibid, 1943, p. 19.
[40] Ibid, 1943, p. 50.
[41] Ibid, 1932, p. 33.
[42] Ibid, 1943, p. 50.

VIII. THE PASTORS

There has been a large number of lay church workers who have done heroic work in behalf of the Kingdom of God and therefore deserve special mention; but because of circumstances we are unable to present their biographies. Instead, we desire to quote a historian when he says: "The old Swedish peasants who arrived here more than a half century ago went into the wilderness and built small, bare buildings of rough trees or of sod, cleared the land and laid the foundation for the church and community life rooted in Christianity. These people were often ignored and considered of little account, but we are beginning to realize that were it not for their sacrifices, courage, labors, patience and their Christian view of life our Swedish colonies would not have been what they are today." [1]

Again we read: "The Minnesota Conference has always been aware of the local needs . . . The pioneer pastors were in the true sense of that word missionaries. They traveled continuously to visit settlements and to preach to our Swedish Lutheran people and to bring them into congregations." [2] We may here repeat the words of the apostle Paul: "And I will most gladly spend and be spent for you," 2 Cor. 12:15.

The annals of the Conference present a list of earnest, consecrated pastors who offered their lives on the altar of the Lord. We shall present very brief biographies of a few from the earlier decades.

Jonas Magney

We have already seen this home missionary in his travels among his countrymen. Of him Dr. Norelius writes: "Since early in October, 1858, I have known Jonas Magney. He had

125

then arrived from Sweden in company with his mother, two brothers, a sister and his stepfather, the well-known Håkan Svedberg in Chisago Lake. He was then in his seventeenth year. It was at the time of the organization of the Minnesota Conference, at what is now Center City, Minnesota. Even though young he took deep interest in the meetings and before my soul's eye there still stands the kind, young man with red, healthy cheeks, who ran errands and served us all wherever there was a need. His burning desire was to promote the Kingdom of God. Where others stood looking on, he went to work on his own accord and was always busy. I saw in him even then the good material of a worker in our Swedish Lutheran vineyard in America. When I at the decision of the Conference started a school in Red Wing, Magney was there as one of the students. During the fall term he was the only student, during the spring term there were ten." [3] "He formed a part of the professor's household, paying one dollar a month for his room and seventy-five cents a week for board. The pastor's study was the first lecture room and tuition was free; when the faculty was called away on other missions, perhaps for a day at a time, the student body would indulge in athletic exercises in the form of wood chopping." [4]

He was ordained at the Synodical meeting in Andover, Illinois, 1870, upon a call from the church at Vasa, Minnesota, as assistant pastor. The pastor of the church, E. Norelius, writes: "During the time he was my assistant I can testify that he served faithfully with the talents the Lord had given him. In doctrine and confession he was a faithful Lutheran; in living he was correct, patient, willing to serve and content with his lot." [5]

Though called to be assistant to the pastor at Vasa, it seems that he spent most of his time traveling in the interest of home missions. In 1870 he traveled three months in Stearns, Douglas and Otter Tail counties. The following year he spent six months in the northwest borderland. And traveling was at that time—as we have seen and know—very difficult, strenuous and dangerous.

In May, 1872, Pastor Magney accepted a call to the church at Cannon Falls, Minnesota, where he was the first resident pastor. Here he built a church and parsonage and also "strengthened the spiritual church." In 1875 he was called to gather funds for the Gustavus Adolphus College at St. Peter, Minnesota. "He succeeded in his work and received only about half the salary offered him." "It was therefore not too much," adds his biographer, "that the Board of Directors gave him as remuneration the honorary doctor's degree."

Later he served Svea and Tabor, Wisconsin; South Stillwater, Minnesota; Balsam, Wisconsin; and Carlton, Minnesota.

J. P. Lundblad

"If you saw him in his home or at a church meeting in his very common attire, you undoubtedly did not realize what was in him. But the moment he came into the pulpit no one was uncertain of his talents. The full, pleasant voice, modulated according to the content of the message, the clear enunciation, the natural gestures, the facial expressions—all tended to charm and impress the listeners. In his spiritual life he was a child of the wonderful seasons of refreshing which visited our fatherland in the middle of last century." Thus the biographer pictures the man who was the first resident pastor of the Red River Valley Conference.[6]

Pastor Lundblad was born in Lund, Sweden, September 12, 1829. From early childhood his desire and longing was towards the ministry, but on account of poverty he dismissed the thought and took up blacksmithing as an apprentice. One day while at work he heard a traveling missionary repeat, with special emphasis, the words: "Unless ye are born again, ye cannot see the Kingdom of God." The words struck him as a sharp arrow. He had read the verse before many times, but now it became a two-edged sword which struck him down before the Lord. Not until he attended the famous Wanneberga meetings (see note) and listened to A. Ahnfeldt, did he find peace to his soul.[7] The pastor in Vinslof, Karl Bergman, instructed him and he went out as a colporteur.

In 1864 he immigrated to America. Here he saw the spiritual needs of the people and began to preach. He went to Paxton, Illinois, where he studied and was ordained at the Synodical meeting in Decorah, Iowa, in 1866, on a call to the church at Marine, Minnesota. He served parishes at Mariedahl, Kansas; Nest Lake and Mamrelund, Minnesota; Parkers Prairie and Fahlun, Minnesota, which was his last pastorate. He also served a large number of settlements in the vicinity of his last parish.

He died February 12, 1900, and is buried in the cemetery of the First Lutheran church, Parkers Prairie. The congregation erected a monument upon his grave. The immortal monument is the shepherd work performed. "And they that are wise shall shine as the brightness of the firmament; and they that turn many to righteousness as the stars for ever and ever," Dan. 12:3.

Louis Johnson

Pastor Louis Johnson was born in Olmstad, Sweden, September 23, 1838, and died at Kensington, Minnesota, March 12, 1912. Upon his arrival in America he took up farming as his occupation. As an indication of the primitive farming methods and personal thrift it may be mentioned that he cut, with the help of his brother, ninety acres of wheat by hand.

His education was limited to one year under the tutorship of Pastor A. Jackson. The teacher said that his pupil "had good sense and good ability to preach." When the congregation at Tripolis, Minnesota, was organized in 1859, Louis Johnson was elected deacon. He often assisted his pastor "both in the home congregation and in the outlying mission fields."[8] In 1872 he was granted a license to preach and in 1879 he was ordained into the holy ministry. For some time he was assistant to Pastor Peter Beckman. His active ministry was mainly in Douglas and Otter Tail counties. He was ordained on a call to Oscar Lake, Wennersborg and Norunga. Later he served Parkers Prairie and Fergus Falls parishes.

Though his academic preparation for the ministry was quite limited he was taught by the Spirit of God and was eager to bring the Gospel message to his countrymen. He used well the talents God had given him.

S. J. Kronberg

Pastor S. J. Kronberg was born in Kyrkhult, Knäred, Sweden, May 11, 1840, the youngest of ten children. His mother died when he was only two and a half years old. "I remember, as it were a dream, from the last day of my mother, how she lay in bed and tearfully looked at me." At the age of twenty-eight Kronberg immigrated to America. He worked in and around Moline, Illinois, a year and then entered Augustana College at Paxton, Illinois, in 1869. During the fall term he went through some very definite and violent spiritual struggles, but found peace with his God.

He was ordained in 1874 on a call to the Christine Lake—Eagle Lake pastorate, Minnesota. His field was "sixty miles square"; at times he served a number of additional parishes during vacancies. He remained in the Christine Lake parish until his retirement in 1904. He died January 3, 1925.

Mr. Kronberg was a talented pastor who broke the bread of life with emphasis and the unction of the Holy Spirit. There were great revivals in his and neighboring parishes during his ministry. In debate he defended the doctrines of the Lutheran Church and always stood on the Rock foundation of the Word of God. Roads and weather never detained him from his appointments.

In his book, "Banbrytaren"—The Pioneer—he describes his acceptance of the call. "A newly organized congregation usually turned to the Conference or Synod for advice in the calling of a pastor. That was the case with the congregation we now have in mind. They appealed to the Conference which in turn promised to help and thus called a theological student. He accepted the call. The pastor was also to spend as much time as possible on the neighboring mission fields. His field was to be Hööks, Himle and Villans (Douglas, Otter Tail and Grant) counties. He had therefore adequate space for his activities.

"The candidate received the call two days before his graduation. He had therefore not much hope of being ordained that year. Hasselquist insisted that he should go to the southwest, but a few old pastors ("prästgubbar") were determined that he should go out to the wild northwest—and so it was decreed. Poor me—was naturally the last in line. Not without worry did he await what was coming.

"While he was waiting to be called before the Ministerium an old pastor from the northwest put his hand on his shoulder and said, 'If the Ministerium should suggest, that you continue another year at the Seminary, then know that that is not the intention of the Ministerium nor do we pastors in the northwest expect it.'

"The question arose in the Ministerium and the candidate answered about as follows: 'As far as returning to the Seminary I have nothing against that, even if it were for five years. But as it is, I am quite up in years and my health is poor. If the honorable Ministerium does not see fit to ordain me, it has a perfect right to do so, but I think that in that case I would rather pay up my school debts and go out west and take a homestead.' That was the nail that drew. ("Detta var skruven.")

"The candidate knew nothing about the west, except that it was big, big, big. . . .

"At the station was a middle aged man to meet the pastor. He had a team of good horses and a new lumber wagon with box. The driver and a pastor rode in the spring seat while the newly ordained pastor sat on a box in the wagon. Every once in a while they would look back and ask: 'How goes it with our new pastor?' " [9]

The "new" pastor fared well in spite of the pioneer trials. He gave a long, active and fruitful ministry in this field. In his book is a picture of the buggy in which he traveled 200,000 miles.

J. O. Cavallin

Pastor J. O. Cavallin was born in Svensköp, Skåne, Sweden, November 25, 1844, and came to America at the age of eighteen, in company with his mother. He entered St. Ansgar's Academy, continued at Paxton, Illinois. He was ordained in 1870 with J. Magney and J. Auslund. His first charge was Spring Garden, where he served from 1870-1880. He spent eighteen months in Austin, Texas, where he organized the church work. During the period of 1880 to 1890 he was pastor of the Bethesda church, Moorhead, Minnesota, and served as part time missionary in the Red River Valley and North Dakota. From 1890 to 1906 he divided his time between Ortonville-Clinton parish; Zion, Minneapolis, and the congregation at Braham, Minnesota. After that he was home missionary in North Dakota and for a while was assistant to the pastor in Moorhead. "In youth he took active part in the external affairs of the church, but because of his natural tendencies and his democratic principles belonged to the minority party, which —however—was recognized at times at the election of officers." [10]

Pastor Cavallin was for many years a regular contributor to the church press, principally reporting on his experiences and observations on the mission fields where he was working.

L. A. Hocanzon

Pastor L. A. Hocanzon was born in Nysund, Orebro län, Sweden, April 22, 1837. From early childhood he had to work very hard. He wanted to be a pastor, but instead he was compelled to follow his father as a carpenter apprentice. He was a child of the spiritual revivals which swept Sweden the middle part of the nineteenth century. At the age of twenty-eight he was converted. In 1862 he was married and seven years later he and his wife came to America. When they came to Lake City, Hocanzon had only fifty cents in his pocket.

He was ordained in 1871 and his first pastorate was Vista, Wauseka County, Minnesota, 1871-1877. He served Cocato, Minn. 1877-1882; Beckville-Litchfield-Dassel-Swan Lake, Minn. 1883-1891; West Duluth-Cloquet-Carlton, Minn., 1892-1895; Emanuel, Merriam Park-Bethesda, St. Paul, Minn., 1895-1900; Butte and mission fields in Montana, 1900-1902; traveled for home mission, 1902-3; was city missionary in St. Paul and Minneapolis, Minn., and pastor at Hastings, Minn., 1903-1919. He died May 21, 1919.

Pastor Hocanzon organized seventeen congregations—two in Texas, two in Montana, one in Iowa and twelve in Minnesota—and superintended the building of eighteen churches.

A biographer describes him as "sincere, strong in faith, sanctified in life, experienced in the school of suffering and also in the glorious guidance of God; rich in universal and brotherly love; conscientious; practical as spiritual counsellor; indefatigable as pastor; interesting as preacher; sincere; deep; happy as husband and father." [11]

"L. A. Hocanzon—a venerable and sturdy pioneer—having done yeoman service in our Synod for forty-seven years; always faithful to his trust, at the cost of sacrifice. His special contribution is to the cause of inner missions. He has exerted a marked influence for good in ever widening circles; he retains a youthful and vigorous mind in spite of advanced age, keeping well abreast of the times in his own field of labor and in matters of common interest." These were the words spoken at the time when he received the honorary degree, D.D., May 27, 1918.[12]

Peter Sjoblom

Pastor Peter Sjoblom was born in Snöstorp parish, Sweden, March 17, 1834, "in a little cottage behind a big rock on the seacoast of Halland." He prepared himself for the profession of teacher and studied at the Schiller School in Gothenberg. While attending school he met P. Fjellstedt and P. Wieselgren.

He came to America in 1866 and was ordained the same year. He served parishes at Bayleytown, Indiana, 1866-1869; Red Wing, Minn., 1869-1889. Other parishes which he served were Brainerd, Minn., Fergus Falls, Minn., Wakefield, Nebr., and Dunnell, Minn. He retired in 1902 and died January 24, 1909.

"Perhaps no person," writes Dr. Emil Lund, "has had a greater bearing on the development of our Church than Pastor Sjoblom. Few have had his ability and gift to counsel in such a simple, straightforward and convincing way with earnest seeking souls." [13]

J. H. Randahl

Pastor J. H. Randahl was born in Lekåsa, Västergötland, Sweden, December 12, 1850. He came from a very pious home. The family immigrated to America in 1858 and settled in West Union, Carver county, Minnesota. He began his studies at St. Ansgar Academy and continued at Augustana College, Paxton, Illinois. He was ordained in 1879. He married Sofia Peterson from Rock Island, Ill.

His first parish was Beaver Valley, S. Dak. The first year he served there the grasshoppers took all the crop, causing great hardships among the people. He moved next to Boone, Iowa; from there to Sioux Falls, S. Dak., 1882-1891; then to Scandia Grove, Minn., 1891-1905; then to Providence Valley, Minn., 1905-1910. In the year 1910 he was called by the Minnesota Conference as home missionary. His annual reports to the Minnesota and Red River Valley Conferences reveal a great concern for souls and a willingness to give his all to the work before him. There were times when he had up to sixteen preaching places. "On one of his last trips," we read, "he traveled in severe weather twelve miles on an old wood sled" in order to bring the message of salvation in Christ to his countrymen. He died May 18, 1924.

L. P. Lundgren

Pastor L. P. Lundgren was born in Essunga, Skaraborgs län, Sweden, March 2, 1851. He lost his father at the age of four and his mother when he was thirteen. At the latter age he went to school three months. At eighteen he immigrated to America. Here he lived at first in Carver county, Minnesota, as a farmer. Later he went south where he experienced much sickness and was near death. At the age of thirty he enrolled at Gustavus Adolphus College and was one of the eight first graduates from that school.[14]

He was ordained in 1892 and became pastor of the Fridhem -Saron pastorate, Hallock, Minnesota. He served this pastorate, which at times also included Red River, Sikar and Tabitha congregations, for a period of thirty-one years. During the first fifteen years he was home missionary in Kittson, Roseau and Marshall counties, Minnesota, besides some work in Canada and North Dakota. He traveled 6,700 miles by rail, 21,000 by horse and 41,000 by automobile. May 28, 1896, he married Alma H. Lund. He died June 14, 1926.

L. P. Stenstrom

When Pastor S. J. Kronberg went to Pelican Rapids to conduct a business meeting January 26, 1878, he had with him a student, L. P. Stenstrom, who had recently arrived from Sweden. Mr. Stenstrom preached his first sermon in the A. F. Sjostrom home in November, 1879.

Pastor L. P. Stenstrom was born in Hangvar parish, Gottland, Sweden, June 18, 1843. He married Julia C. Sandstrom of Visby in 1866 and six years later they immigrated to America. After some period of study he was sent, as mentioned, as a catechist to the Elizabeth, Central Swede Grove, Gotalund (Amor) and Fergus Falls field. In 1881 he was ordained on the recommendation of the Minnesota Conference and upon a call to the above mentioned parish. He served the parish (Pelican Rapids and Elizabeth) continuously for a period of nearly four decades—his entire ministry. The parish was divided in 1919 and he continued to serve the congregation at Elizabeth until 1920.

He died on Easter Sunday, April 9, 1926. "He was a true Christian, a man of sterling character, sympathetic, kindhearted, devoted in heart and soul to his work." [15]

References

[1] Lund, Dr. Emil. Minnesota Konferensens Historia, p. 64.
[2] Korsbaneret, 1909, p. 149.
[3] Ibid, 1911, p. 196.
[4] Johnson, Dr. Emeroy, A Church Planted, p. 317.
[5] Korsbaneret, 1911, p. 196.
[6] Ibid, 1901, p. 133.
[7] Wanneberga was a hill in northern Skane, Sweden, where great outdoor meetings—camp meetings— were held during the period of the great revivals in the first part of the 1880s. The meetings were under the direction of the free movement (Covenant). See "En Kyrkans brytningstid in nordskansk bygd" in Lund Stifts Julbok, 1935.
[8] Johnson, Dr. Emeroy, A Church Planted, p. 224.
[9] Kronberg, Banbrytaren, pp. 129-132
[10] Minnesskrift, p. 186. The article from which this quotation is taken is in reality an autobiography, since J.O.C. is the author.
[11] Lund, Dr. Emil, Minnesota Konferensens Historia, pp. 105-106.
[12] Korsbaneret, 1920, p. 167.
[13] Lund, Dr. Emil. op. cit., p. 208.
[14] Korsbaneret, 1927, p. 261.
[15] History of the Central Swede Grove church, July 1-3, 1949.

IX. AUXILIARY ORGANIZATIONS

Anniversary Notes

"The women that publish the tidings are a great host."
Psalms 68:11.

The women of the pioneer days deserve special mention. They carried their part of the burdens and many were real heroines. They shared in the toil and the prayers which went into the building of the early churches. They inspired and supported the men in their work.

As the women of the First Easter day heard Jesus say: "Come and see . . . go and tell," so the women of the Red River Valley Conference have not only been faithful listeners to the Gospel, but have "published the tidings." They have not only supported the work of the local church, but have greatly undergirded the home and foreign mission program.

On the Fortieth Anniversary we salute the women who have carried the message of the Cross, either as leaders and officers or rank and file soldiers in the army of the Lord. Many have finished their earthly journey. Peace be upon their memory! Others are among the "host" who "go and tell," because they have "seen."

Before we take a look at the history of the mission-minded women and children we shall let a few representatives speak "out of their hearts."

Greetings From Former Conference Presidents

It gives me a great pleasure in sending this greeting for your fortieth anniversary. When I look back at the little mustard seed that was planted forty years ago, it makes my heart rejoice to see what a wonderful tree it has become.

God bless all faithful workers in the Red River Valley Conference in their continued loyal service of the Lord, Jesus Christ.

Sincerely,

Mrs. Alma Lundgren, President, 1913-1914.

* * *

The Women's Missionary Society of the Red River Valley Conference has always been very dear to me. Beginning a new venture of faith in God's Kingdom is always a challenge and a matchless opportunity. God has nurtured and directed our united efforts for the extension of His work and He will continue to do so always. Jh. 10:16.

In His service,

Mrs. S. W. Swenson, President, 1914-1918.

* * *

Jh. 6:35. The Bread of Life. The Red River Valley has often been called the Breadbasket of the Northwest. So it is very fitting that the W.M.S. of the Red River Valley Conference should do its share to bring the "Bread of Life" to many souls throughout the world. I pray that God may continue to bless your efforts as He has these forty years.

Sincerely,

Mrs. James Moody, President, 1918-1924.

* * *

Studying, with interest, your reports I know that the Christ-love in the hearts of many of your members has laid hold, in faith, upon the promises of God—the results are rewarding. May we all make our every act count toward our mutual goal of winning more souls for Heaven. "The love of Christ constraineth us." 2 Cor. 5:14.

Sincerely,

Mrs. Walfred Erickson, President, 1924-1928; 1930-1935.

There are two passages of Scripture that stand out in my memory of past W.M.S. working days as well as in the efforts today. Maybe because they are precious in my own life. Jer. 33:3 and Eph. 3:20—"great and mighty things, which thou knowest not," and "abundantly above all that we ask or think." May these promises become real to us. May God's blessings be with you in remembering these past forty years.

Mrs. George Standish, President, 1929.

For five years I had the privilege to serve as Conference President. I thank God for this opportunity.

I would like to give a tribute to my former co-workers in thankfulness and appreciation. Many have moved out of our Conference and others have passed to their reward. The ranks have been filled by younger women. Membership has increased.

My prayer is that God will continue to bless our work. "Go, labor on."

Sincerely,
Mrs. Adin Nelson, President, 1935-1940.

* * *

Evaluation of the Women's Missionary Society of the R.R. V. Conference:

For forty years the Women's Missionary Society has labored and served. It is with gratitude to God that we remember our founders and the early pioneers to whom the cause of missions was dear.

God has blessed the work through the years, memberships and contributions have increased until we now have 106 Societies with a membership of 2,395, including Adult, Business Women and Teen-agers, and the 66 Junior organizations. Contributions the first year were $429.06, in 1952 they amounted to $26,382.70, a total through the years of approximately $329,-000.00.

In the early years of our history a sum of money was set aside as an encouragement to students who were studying for the ministry. Help was also given to Home Mission congregations in our Conference. Recently a gift of $3,000.00 was given to the newly organized Messiah church in Fargo, North Dakota.

Generous contributions have been given to Conference Home Missions and Conference Charities as well as fulfilling our obligations to all branches of the work as recommended by the Synodical Society.

May God continue to bless our labors to His glory and the extension of His Kingdom.

Mrs. Ernest Nelson, Historian.

The Women's Missionary Society

A meeting of delegates and other interested women was held in the Swedish Lutheran Church, Warren, Minnesota, March 15, 1913. Mrs. L. P. Lundgren was the convener and the purpose was the organization of a Woman's Home and Foreign Missionary Society within the Red River Valley Conference. The meeting was held at the request of the president of the Synodical organization. In her introductory remarks Mrs. Lundgren pointed to the fact that the women of a number of Conferences had organized and affiliated with the national organization and many thousand dollars had been gathered for home and foreign missions.[1] The attention was also called to the fact that as a Conference we have large fields to care for, many small congregations which need support, many places where the people are living without the Means of Grace.

A motion was adopted, that a Woman's Home and Foreign Missionary Society be organized. A constitution—sic, "trans-

139

lated into Swedish"—changed to fit a smaller organization, was adopted.[2] There were sixty ladies present and nearly all joined as active members.

Article II states the purpose: "To awaken greater interest for the cause of missions and to foster a true missionary spirit among the women, youth and children, that they by the Grace of God, may obey the divine command, 'Go and make disciples of all the nations.'" Greetings were read from the president of the Synodical Society, Mrs. Emmy Evald, and the president of the Minnesota Conference Society, Miss Hilvine Franzen.

Officers elected were: President, Mrs. L. P. Lundgren, Hallock, Minn.; Vice President, Mrs. O. E. Abrahamson, Warren, Minn.; Secretary, Mrs. J. M. Persenius, Grand Forks, N. Dak.; Treasurer, Mrs. N. E Bystrom, Warren, Minn.; Corresponding Secretary, Mrs. J. Moody, Fertile, Minn.

District presidents were: Alexandria, Mrs. A. J. Ostrom, Evansville, Minn.; Fargo, Mrs. H. S. Chilgren, Herby, N. D.; Red River, Mrs. F. N. Anderson, Warren, Minn.

Items of business at the first meeting included a request that "our Society be excused from sending a delegate to the meeting of the Synodical Society this year; that the permission be asked to publish the record of the proceedings in the printed minutes of the Conference; that appreciation be expressed to the First Church, Warren, for kindness and hospitality; and that "we adjourn to accept an invitation from the Conference to a welcome reception."

From here we quote: "The festivities began with the hymn (Hemlandssång, "Till verksamhet") 196. Scripture reading and prayer by Pastor O. Wallin. After that addresses of inspiration and encouragement by the Pastors G. Wahlund, P. E. Ording, Carl Solomonson, and F. N. Anderson, who all welcomed us to the Conference, church and communities, called attention to the great home and foreign mission fields." [3] Thus the flag was hoisted and the "bon voyage" was expressed as this "sister" ship launched out on its way.

The Society seems to have "gone right to bat" for the Kingdom of God. There was much activity from the very start. At the first annual meeting the president reported, that the "constitution does not fully outline the duties of the officers, wherefore they have to decide matters according to their best judgment and the Grace of God." [4]

There were seventeen Societies that joined the first year. Total receipts were $429.06, and disbursements $206.76. Important forward-looking resolutions were adopted: appeal for the mission in Puerto Rico; a representative in every congregation for the Mission Tidings; coffee festivals for home mission during the month of March; that Dr. Betty Nilsson be invited to make a speaking tour through the Conference.

New projects were added from year to year. Besides the regular contributions for mission at home and abroad there were special causes, such as the Red Cross, European and China Relief, Harry Soxie, Eskimo studying at the Lutheran Bible Institute. Special assistance was given for the salary of the pastor at Thief River Falls; support was given to the building projects at Hines, Swift, Graceton, Salol and Spooner. From 1920 until the new mission plan of the Augustana Church came into being, the Society gave from $800 to $1,200 annually for home mission. For a period of five years special assistance was given to a worthy student with the ministry in view.[5] On one occasion the Society gave $25.00 to each of two students serving on the home mission fields along the Canadian border, so that they could buy themselves new suits of clothes.

The total income of the Missionary Society from 1913 to 1952 amounts to $329,000.00. "Our interest in home mission is revealed in the money gathered, yet our zeal for the lost and deserted ought to be increased. If our churches do not grow and new congregations are not organized our church will soon be but a memory." [6]

The Red River Valley Conference has not only given money for the Kingdom of God, but it has also given laborers. We believe the Women's Missionary Society has been instrumental in kindling the missionary spirit in hearts of many consecrated workers. Thus a large number of missionaries have gone forth from this Conference and labored on the foreign fields: Dr. and Mrs. Olof Olson, Battle Lake; Dr. Lillian Olson, Bertha, Minn.; Alice K. Anderson, Clearbrook, Minn.; Lois Bernhardson, Comstock, Minn.; Stella Carlson, Hallock, Minn.; Sadie Josephson, Bismarck, N.D.; Alice Turnblad, Sebeka, Minn.; Edith Kjellin, Gwinner, N. Dak.

Six deaconesses have come from our Conference, namely, Sr. Ingeborg Nystul, Goodrich, Minn.; Sr. Lillie Jackson, Fergus Falls, Minn.; Sr. Irene Danielson, Hallock, Minn.; Sr. Minnie Carlson and Sr. Gertrude Carlson, both of Stephen, Minn., and Sr. Vera Nelson, Mohall, N. Dak.

The primary aim of the Society was to enroll the local societies and to enlist the women as active workers.[7] The reports to the annual meetings speak of gains and losses. Though there has been retrogression momentarily now and then the organization has experienced gradual progress. At the end of the first decade the Society had an adult membership of 1092, in 1933 it was 1099, in 1942 it had increased to 1363. In 1943 the North Dakota District was added to the Conference, boosting the membership of the Society to 1489. In 1952 the adult membership had reached 2,040. Of these 718 were in the Alexandria District, 132 in Bemidji, 343 in Dakota, 337 in Fargo, and 718 in Red River.

Getting subscriptions for the Mission Tidings has been the object of both work and worry during the history of the Society. In the second year there were 303 subscribers within the

Conference, the next year 410, in 1922 there were 833 and in 1951 there were 1352.

During these forty years the Society has had eight presidents, as follows: Mrs. L. P. Lundgren, 1913-1914; Mrs. S. W. Swenson, 1914-1918; Mrs. James Moody, 1918-1924; Mrs. Walfred Erickson, 1924-1928; Mrs. George Standish, 1929; Mrs. Walfred Erickson, 1930-1935; Mrs. Adin Nelson, 1935-1940; Mrs. Oscar O. Gustafson, 1940-1952; Mrs. Anton Chell, 1952-.

The Young Women's Society

In 1925 the president of the Women's Missionary Society in her report mentioned that "in many places the need for a Senior or Young People's Band has been felt" in order to keep the "teen age" interested. "The First Lutheran church at Roseau has met this by organizing a Junior Brotherhood. Grand Forks has upon request of its older Juniors organized a Senior Band. Others will do the same. No leader will say 'no you can't belong any longer.' The Young People's Mission Band is a natural result."[8]

However, there had been missionary activity among the young women before this, though not officially reported or connected with the Conference organization. A Young Women's Missionary Society was organized in McIntosh in 1916, another in Moorhead in 1920, in Clearbrook 1926, Grand Forks and Parkers Prairie 1927.[9] Mrs. A. W. Spaeth, Evansville, Minn., was elected Young Women's Secretary.[10] The following year Mrs. A. L. Peterson, Evansville, Minn., became Secretary and the resolutions on organization of Y.W.M.S. was repeated. Mission studies were urged and treasure chests were recommended for the raising of money. In the next annual report the president of the Conference Society could report ten Young Women's Societies with a membership of ninety-four. "We are happy over the increased interest in this department."[11]

143

In 1931 the report of the Secretary for this department was included in the printed minutes. The next year Delphine Lindahl, the secretary, reports that two more Societies had been added and the income was $243.80 in this branch of the work. The membership in the Y.W.M.S. for the Conference has been: 1933, 148; 1935, 183; 1937, 201; 1940, 255; 1942, 217; 1943, 226; 1945, 236; 1947, 265; 1948, 279; 1950, 325; 1951, 378.

The Junior Missionary Society

The Junior work started very gradually—almost as when a child begins to crawl and finally walks.

Thus it was resolved—in 1916—that we "continue with mite boxes in the Sunday Schools so that the children have a chance to give for the children's hospital ward on the foreign field";[12] and the president asks "if we cannot in our Conference put more forces to work through so-called Junior work";[13] and the Junior Secretary, Miss Esther Rosenthal reported briefly on "Junior work";[14] "that we continue with the saving banks in the Sunday Schools."[15] The president reports in 1919 that even though there had been no Junior Secretary during the previous year many members had been won. "This work is important and should be taken up in all the congregations, because if we do not train the missionary spirit among our children we cannot expect them to continue this work when we are gone. May we therefore elect a Junior Secretary."[16] In 1925 it was decided to elect a Junior Secretary for each District.[17]

The Minutes of 1920 mention that the Junior Secretary, Mrs. A. B. Anderson, read her report on Junior work.[18] The next year the president reports that there were 189 Juniors. A Junior Mission Band had been organized in Moorhead with 60 members and there had been missionary activity among the Juniors in many places.[19] In 1922 there were, according to the report of the president, 506 Juniors,[20] but the Junior Secretary

144

Mrs. Oscar O. Gustafson
Treasurer of the W. M. S.
20 years and President 12
years.

Mrs. Anton Chell
President W. M. S. 1952-

Executive Board   Women's Missionary Society.

Front, left to right: Mrs. Ernest Nelson, Historian; Mrs. Clinton
Lundgren, Secr.; Mrs. Anton Chell, President; Mrs. Roland Borene,
1st V. P.; Mrs. R. Araskog, Treas.; Mrs. Vendel Olson, 2nd V. P.;
Mrs. Eskil Bostrom, Corr. Secr.

Second row: Mrs. Alfred Sylling, Dakota Dist. Pres.; Mrs. Ed Wal-
lin, My Missionary for a Day, Secr.; Mrs. Adin Nelson, Lit. Secr.;
Mrs. O. G. Berg, Industrial Secr.; Mrs. Conrad Lund, Statistician;
Mrs. M. Mosbeck, R. R. Dist. Pres.: Mrs. Ted Ranstrom, M. Tidings
Secr.; Mrs. Hugo Magnuson, Am. Mission Secr.; Mrs. W. Blomquist,
B. W. & Teen Agers Secr.

Not on picture: Miss Mabel Olson, Children's Div. Secr.

—who for the first time has her report in the printed minutes—reports 686. In 1924 there were 24 organized Junior Mission Bands with 894 members in the Conference, distributed as follows: Alexandria District, nine Bands with 336 members; Red River, nine Bands with 552 members; Fargo, four Bands with 160 members; Bemidji, two Bands with 46 members. This seems to have been the peak year in the Junior membership. In her report 1951 the president says that "Juniors are not counted by membership, all Junior Societies or Sunday Schools contributing to the Thankoffering and Friendship Funds are listed as active organizations. We have Junior Societies as follows: Alexandria District 21, Bemidji 4, Dakota 8, Fargo 8, Red River 19." [21]

The Juniors have been interested in a great many phases of the work of the Church at home and abroad. They have supported the mission work in Africa, China, India, and have contributed for the home mission work and charity. For instance in the Secretary's report, 1923, there are nineteen different causes mentioned.[22] But the importance of the Junior work is not only expressed in projects and money gathered and given. "What a hope for the future when they (the children) shall take their places not only as contributors, but also as workers, Junior work shall not have been in vain. There will be someone from the ranks of the Juniors who will be moved by the special appeal of the world's greatest need, the Gospel of Christ,[23] and give himself as a full-time missionary."

The first Junior Secretary was appointed in 1916 by the executive committee[24] "to work up interest among the children and youth where such work is feasible." Miss Esther Rosenthal seems to have been appointed.[25] In 1918 the executive committee of the Conference was asked to interest, as far as time and opportunity would permit, the children and youth to be members in the Junior department of the Missionary Society.[26] The next year the president urges that a Junior Secretary be elected and Mrs. A. B. Anderson, Evansville, was chosen.[27] Since then the following have served as Junior Secretaries: Mrs. Carl Johnson, Moorhead, Minn., 1921; Mrs. P. J. Holmberg, Grand Forks, N. D., 1922-1931; Mrs. Clarence Hall, Fergus Falls, Minn., 1931-1935; Mrs. Roger Anderson, Lake Park, Minn., 1935-1938; Mrs. Karl Nelson, Lancaster, Minn., 1938-1942; Mrs. Ingham Idso, Amenia, N. D., 1942-1947; Miss Mabel Olson, Bismarck, N. D., 1947-1951.

In 1950 the name Junior Missionary Society was changed to Children's Division of the Women's Missionary Society. Latest records show a total of sixty-five children's organizations within the Conference, with an approximate membership of 3,500 and a yearly offering for missions amounting to $4000.

The Luther League

The work among and for the young people weighed heavily upon the hearts of the leaders of the Conference from the very first. "We have in most of the congregations active and well-behaved Young People's Societies, which are willing to do all in their power in supporting the Conference and Synod" and the suggestion was therefore made that "a Conference Luther League perhaps ought to be organized, so that real great festivities could be held with our beloved youth." [28] Later reports state that "the young people are good and industrious," in "many congregations are active Bible classes"; but the "programs at the Young People's meetings are not what we would wish them to be." [29] "When father goes to lodge and mother goes to club, the young are left in the street." [30]

Meanwhile District organizations were effected in many sections of the Conference—in the Bismarck District, July 13-15, 1918, and the Sheyenne District in 1921.[31]

At the Conference meeting, 1921, Dr. S. M. Miller addressed the Convention and $50 was appropriated for the Lutheran Bible Institute. The president of the Conference reports, that "the Bible Schools and the interest in them reveals

that God has means within our Church to save the youth." [32]
The following year we read that "a Conference League has
come into existence, and its program is Bible study";[33] and
that Bible Conferences had been held at Northwestern College
and North Star College. The following year a resolution was
passed that each District be represented on the Luther League
Bible Institute committee by one pastor and one layman.[34]

In 1925 the following resolution was received from the
Synodical Luther League through its president, Pastor Conrad Bergendoff, and was adopted by the Conference: "That, if
possible, one evening session at each annual meeting of the
Conference be devoted to the consideration of the young people's organizations and their work in the church." [35]

It is evident that the Bible study movement as represented
in the Lutheran Bible Institute gave impetus and direction
to the work among the youth, but the work was conducted
on District levels.

In 1931 the Conference recommended that the District officers meet and discuss the possibility of organizing a Conference League. The Luther League Council was organized at
a meeting held in the Trinity Lutheran church, Detroit Lakes,
Minn., August 30, 1932. Pastor Carl A. E. Gustafson, Elbow
Lake, Minn., was elected president; Miss Luverne Cook, Haw-
ley, Minn., secretary; Wallace Carlson, Eagle Bend, Minn.,
treasurer; Pastor Harry L. Sjogren, Thief River Falls, Minn,
statistician.

The stated purpose of the Council was to "unite the young
people of our church in order to promote the study of the
Word of God, the history, confessions and the missionary activities of the church, to assist in educational work and develop among them a deeper spiritual, intellectual and Christian
fellowship." [36] The Council was "the medium through which
the District may promote a common cause." [37] It was to serve

as "an intermediary between the local League and the Synodical Luther League Council." [38]

The Bemidji District was received into the Council in 1935 and North Dakota in 1942. The Council sponsored the Fair Hills Bible Camp, Detroit Lakes, Minn., annually from 1934 to 1945. It was also active in other ways. It sent delegates to all the Christian Youth Conferences sponsored by the Augustana League. In 1942 the Council included all six Districts, with 120 Leagues and 4,660 members.

In 1945 the Luther League Council was dissolved and the Luther League work on a Conference basis was reorganized. The various Districts were to arrange their own Bible Camps and a Luther League Convention was to be held annually at some central place. The first annual Convention was held in the Bethesda Lutheran Church, Moorhead, Minn., October 19, 20, 1946. [39] The Red River, Fargo and Alexandria Districts have conducted their Bible Camps at Luther Crest, on Lake Carlos, near Alexandria, Minn.; the Bemidji District at the American Lutheran Camp near Blackduck, Minn.; the North Dakota District at the Pilgrim Camp, Matogoshe, Bottineau, N. D., and at Mt. Carmel, Alexandria, Minn.

The Red River Valley Conference has not only encouraged the Luther League work, but it has included the reports of the Council and League in the regular minutes and not only as appendix. We believe this is symbolic of the attitude of the Conference to the work among and by the youth within its confines.

Lutheran Brotherhood

At the Conference meeting in Fergus Falls, Minn., March 22-26, 1916, the laymen present gathered at "the recommendation of the president" in the basement of the church—simultaneously with the meeting of the Pastoral Conference. Mr. C. C. Holmquist, Lancaster, Minn., conducted devotionals, and Mr. Aug. Lundgren, Warren, Minn., was elected secretary.

It was decided that "we as lay delegates henceforth meet, while the Pastoral Conference is in session, to discuss such matters within our church as may pertain to the furtherance of the work of the congregations." [40] The finance system of the church was the topic at the first session. At the second meeting it was decided to petition the Conference that it requests the congregations to pay the traveling expenses of the pastors and laymen to the Conference meetings. This motion was adopted by the Conference. [41]

The laymen's sessions were held annually and such topics have been discussed as "The Reformation," "Finances," "Home Mission," "Pension Fund," "How Shall We as Laymen Best Promote the Spiritual Life of Our Congregations?" "How Shall We Get More Pastors?" etc. The reports of the laymen's meetings as printed in the official Conference Minutes are examples of secretarial brevity. Several reports have only three lines. One report gives the time for the meeting, the topic: "How Can We Laymen Promote the Furtherance of the Kingdom of God"; three speakers are mentioned by name—all this in three and a half lines. One resolution is worthy of note: "Resolved, that it is the firm conviction of the Laymen's Conference, that interest in the Conference and Synodical work is best promoted by creating interest in the local church and its problems. We firmly believe that if we are right with God, seeking and accepting his Kingdom and righteousness, that interest for Synodical and Conference work will follow, generosity will be engendered and the necessary funds for carrying on the work will be raised." [42]

The first mention of the Brotherhood work is in 1926—in the tenth year of the meetings of the laymen—when we read: "After the discussion Prof. G. Holmquist presented the work and importance of the Lutheran Brotherhood." [43] A year later

"A request was presented from the Augustana Brotherhood toward the expense of that organization." [44] A committee of three was "after due deliberation" appointed "to make an answer." The third year the topic: "How Can We Best Serve the Church?" was discussed and following the discussion Mr. Otto Leonardson "made a talk on the benefits of joining the Lutheran Brotherhood organization." [45]

At the Conference meeting in Fergus Falls, Minn., April 20, 1932, the Laymen's Conference resolved, after some discussion, to organize. "The question of organizing a Conference Brotherhood was discussed. This discussion was followed by a motion by Prof. G. Holmquist and seconded by Mr. Emil Nelson, that the laymen proceed to organize a Lutheran Brotherhood of the Red River Valley Conference. After a prolonged discussion the motion was put to a vote and was declared lost." [46]

At the Conference meeting in Fargo, N. D., April 24-27, 1941, the laymen discussed the topic: "The Lutheran Church and Its Men." Mr. H. A. Smith, treasurer of the Augustana Brotherhood, "presented a motion and moved for its adoption. It was unanimously passed by the assembly." We presume that this resolution was relative to a Brotherhood, because in the printed minutes we find that "in compliance with a resolution originating in the Laymen's Conference, April 24th, recommending the organizing of a Conference Lutheran Brotherhood, the Convention resolved,

That we organize a Lutheran Brotherhood in the Red River Valley Conference; that we adjourn to make the preliminary arrangements for this setup." [47]

In his report to the next Convention the president of the Conference says: "Another evidence of the interest of our men in the affairs of the church is the organization of a Lutheran Brotherhood and a few local Brotherhoods in our congregations. These give our men added opportunity to study the needs of the church and to assist the various institutions and missionary agencies. We anticipate that this will do much to develop latent powers among our men and to encourage them to accept a greater stewardship responsibility." [48] At the meeting of the laymen Dr. J. G. Youngquist, from the Augustana Book Concern, presented the matter of "why a Brotherhood should be organized, its duties and responsibilities, its opportunities to win the unchurched for Christ, its duties to welcome people to attend church services, to work and win the youth for our church and support the Sunday School and Boy Scout movement, and also bring back the lapsed members of our various congregations." [49]

At the organization meeting a constitution was also adopted. H. A. Smith, Elbow Lake, Minn., was elected president; Alfred Holmquist, Hallock, Minn., vice president, and Walter Sundberg, Fergus Falls, Minn., secretary-treasurer. The first Board members were: Alexandria District, Otto Larson, Nelson; Fargo District, W. G. Smellie, Fargo, N. D.; Bemidji District, Emil Nelson, Clearbrook; Red River District, Edgar Mattson, Warren; Bismarck District, Bertil Kjellin, Gwinner, N.D.; Sheyenne District, H. A. Johnson, Sheyenne, N.D.

From 1943 until 1948 the Laymen's meeting and the Lutheran Brotherhood met as two separate groups during the annual Conference Conventions, though some of the business was common to both bodies. Thus a committee was elected at the Laymen's meeting to present nominations for officers to the Brotherhood meeting,[50] which was held the following day. The main and general difference between the Laymen's Conference and the Lutheran Brotherhood was, that the former was a rather informal meeting for the discussion of devotional topics and matter relating to the work of the church in general, while the latter dealt with the objectives and the work of the Brotherhood in particular. However, "all the Conference delegates were declared Brotherhood delegates." [51]

At a meeting of the Brotherhood April 29, 1948, a recommendation from the Board of Trustees was adopted, "requesting a change in the constitution to permit the annual meeting to be held at some other time than at the Red River Valley Conference, so that more time could be devoted to the Brotherhood program." Accordingly a motion was passed that Article V, Section 1, of the constitution be changed to read: "The time for the annual meeting of this organizaiton shall be decided by the Executive Committee."

References

[1] Minutes, R.R.V. Conference, 1913, p. 69.
The first "Women's Missionary Society" in the world was organized in London, 1834, and the "Women's Union Missionary Movement" was launched in America in 1860. A "Woman's Missionary Society" was organized in the Immanuel Church, Chicago, Ill., in 1888 with 200 members. Mrs. Emmy Evald was the leader. At a Synodical meeting at Chisago City, Minn., 1891, it was agreed by a number of women present to meet the next year at Lindsborg, Kansas, to organize a Synodical Society. Several sessions were held and the Society was organized at the Dr. C. A. Swensson home, Lindsborg. A petition was presented to the Synod in session for its sanction. "After a long discussion it was passed by a majority . . . that the Synod express its joy over this Socety and grants to it its undivided approval." "The suspense was over. The women were deeply moved and overjoyed. With hearts aglow they gathered for a season of prayer and thanksgiving." (These Fifty Years, pp. 6, 21, 24.)
Conference Societies had been organized in Illinois, 1900; Nebraska, 1906; Iowa and Minnesota, 1907; New York, 1908; California, 1912, and New England, 1913. In 1909 the Synodical Society had joined the women of Sweden, Denmark, Norway, Finland and Germany in the observance of Advent Prayer Day.
[2] Kvinnornas Hem och Hednamissionsförening, av Augustana Synoden, 1913, p. 8. See Minnesota Stats Tidning, March 26, 1913.
[3] Minutes, R.R.V. Conference, 1913, p. 73.
[4] Ibid, 1914, p. 51. "If a local Society contributes $5, $10 or more to the missions a year, all the members become thereby members in the Synodical organization."
[5] These Fifty Years, p. 157.
[6] Minutes, R.R.V. Conference, 1916, p. 54.
[7] Ibid, 1919, p. 64.
[8] Ibid, 1925, p. 71.
[9] Ibid, 1929, p. 66.
[10] Ibid, 1929, p. 77.
[11] Ibid, 1931, p. 75.
[12] Minutes R.R.V. Conference, 1916, p. 57.
[11] Ibid, 1916, p. 52.
[14] Ibid, 1917, p. 58.
[15] Ibid, 1918, p. 63.
[16] Ibid, 1919, p. 64.
[17] Ibid, 1925, p. 74.
[18] Ibid, 1920, p. 61.
[19] Ibid, 1920, p. 61.
[20] Ibid, 1922, p. 65.
[21] Ibid, 1951, p. 93.
[22] Ibid, 1923, p. 89.
[23] Ibid, 1925, p. 70.
[24] Ibid, 1916, p. 56.
[25] Ibid, 1917, p. 58.

[26] Ibid, 1918, p. 64.
[27] Ibid, 1919, p. 69.
[28] Ibid, 1913, p. 38.
[29] Ibid, 1914, p. 16, 14.
[30] Ibid, 1920, p. 14.
[31] Minutes, Bismarck District, p. 44. Sheyenne District, p. 75.
[32] Minutes, R.R.V. Conference, 1921, p. 15.
[33] Ibid, 1922, p. 15, 59.
[34] Ibid, 1923, p. 75.
[35] Ibid, 1925, p. 54.
[36] Ibid, 1932, p. 48.
[37] Ibid, 1934, p. 43.
[38] Ibid, 1940, p. 55.
[39] Ibid, 1946, p. 55.
[40] Ibid, 1916, p. 49.
[41] Ibid, 1917, p. 53, 51.
[42] Ibid, 1916, p. 61, 62.
[43] Ibid, 1926, p. 62.
[44] Ibid, 1927, p. 63.
[45] Ibid, 1928, p. 63.
[46] Ibid, 1932, p. 56.
[47] Ibid, 1941, p. 97, 66.
[48] Ibid, 1942, p. 16.
[49] Ibid, 1942, p. 85.
[50] Ibid, 1943, p. 90.
[51] Ibid. 1948, p. 68.

X. IN THE PROCESS
By-Products

If you enter a carpentershop you will notice the finished cabinet standing in the center of the room, ready to be moved into some beautiful home. But as you look around on the floor your eyes rest upon small shavings and discarded pieces of wood. They were once part of the material that went into the cabinet, but now they are thrown aside. They were not unimportant. They were perhaps the rugged knots and edges which helped to hold the wood in the vise while it was being fashioned into its perfected and polished form.

In the process of fashioning congregations there were items which at the time were considered of great importance, but which later were found superfluous or even out of place. Every part of the church and its institutions have had some of these oddities.

Looking back to the "rock from which we are hewn"—the church of Sweden—we find stipulations as follows:

"Boys and girls shall not crowd into the pews, but shall stand in the aisles." [1]

"If wives of soldiers or charity patients squeeze themselves into the pews to the annoyance of other women, they shall be fined four cents." [2]

"Sigge Anderson was accepted as marshal ("Spögubbe") whose duty it shall be to keep the people awake and to prevent noise and disturbance." [3]

"Parents whose children do not know Luther's Catechism and Svebelii explanation by heart shall be fined two dollars

154

and shall be required to put their children in school immediately, and if they refuse they (the parents) shall be put in the stock." [4]

"If a person steals lumber from his neighbor he shall, as a punishment, sit in the main aisle of the church during services, holding a tree-twig in his hand." [5]

The pioneers in the daughter church in America encountered problems similar to those of the mother church. Thus we read that "in order that there be no disturbance during the time services are held, the congregation sees fit to impose a fine of fifty cents on anyone bringing dogs along to the meeting place."[6] "Resolved, that one of the deacons sits in the balcony during the services and sees that there is no disturbance.'[7] "Resolved, that no member of the congregation shall talk more than fifteen minutes at a time at the annual meeting." [8] "The janitor shall have a salary of $18 and his duties shall be: to keep the church clean; to show the people where graves shall be dug; meet and stable the pastor's horse; fire properly in the stoves and preserve order." [9] "Pit Bjork shall repair the barn by the church (used for the pastor's horse). He shall put straw on the roof and plaster between the logs; also repair the door; all for a consideration of $2.00." [10] "It is the duty of the members to attend church and annual meetings, since absent members must be satisfied with decisions by those present." [11] "The duty of the sexton shall be, to keep the building clean, warm and in order at all services and for the Sunday School. He shall see to it, that everything goes decently during the services and Sunday School, so that noise and disturbance may not occur within or without the church. Tobacco smoking and spitting on the floor is strictly forbidden." [12] Another church was a little more considerate with the people with tobacco habits because it decided "to have twelve spittoons made and placed in the church, at the cost of twelve cents apiece." [13]

A congregation decided (1888) that the male members each

contribute $3.00 for the payment of the debt on the church and that the "little house back of the church" be paid by means of a fifty-five cent assessment on every female member. The church was to be scrubbed by the folks who had their children in the Swedish school during the summer. The treasurer was to have a salary of one and one-half per cent of the amount of the financial turnover in the church treasury.

In one community a Ladies Aid discussed whether to use the money in the treasury to build a church or a telephone line.[14] In one congregation the "Sunday School was conducted under the leadership of Nils Nylen. The church was considered too sacred a place for it, wherefore the P. E. Dahl home was opened for the children."[15]

Congregational singing was sometimes a problem — and still is. But there was one congregation which was well provided, because "sacristan Dala Per has a voice that can be heard a mile if windows are open." Therefore when a subscription was taken for the purchase of an organ many protested, saying: "Who can play it? Furthermore we have a songmaster."[16] One church stipulated that "children of parents not members of the church, who desire to be confirmed, shall pay five dollars to missions."[17]

The collections were taken by "håfgång." "Håven" was the "offering plate." It consisted of an eight inch deep round bag, tapering towards the bottom from which hung a tassel. It was usually of red or blue velvet, sometimes black, and was fastened to a four foot long handle. The ushers would hold the "håv" before the worshipers, pew after pew. At times the handle had a feather in the end so that the usher could tickle those who were sleeping.

There were other ways in which the pioneer period differed from our times. The conduct of the people was often different from our nervous age. They were calm and composed. They were not rushed, even though the tasks were many and arduous. The people took time for the church. A quotation may illustrate the point. "The day of confirmation 1883 included regular services, examination of the confirmation children, address to the class, communion sermon and communion. It was four o'clock in the afternoon before everything was over, but it was a holiday for all. The pastor did not get nervous if the people looked at their watches, if the children cried, or if the janitor threw out a dog." [18]

A Unique Pulpit

The Spruce Hill congregation has a pulpit which is alone in its class. In originality and workmanship it differs from all pulpits in the Augustana Church. In all probability it is a replica or at least an inspiration from some church in Sweden.

It is coneshaped, designed to stand against the wall in the righthand corner as you look toward the front of the church. Along the upper edge are two lines of panels, each containing a Bible verse carved in the wood. The words and letters are all uniform and in a straight line, as if printed. Each panel has also a border of flower designs. Below these panels are five Bible scenes carved—the birth of Christ—Christ and the Samaritan woman—the triumphal entry—Christ and Nicodemus —the Resurrection. Selected passages from these Bible stories are carved in the same uniform and artistic way above and below the scenes. We give one example:

> *"Och Ängelen sade till dem; warer icke förfärade; si jag bådar eder stor glädje wilket allt folket wederfaras skall."*

> *"And the angel said to them, Be not afraid; for behold, I bring you good news of great joy which will be to all the people."*

The artist was Pehr Christianson, born in Simris parish, Sweden, May 16, 1855. At the age of sixteen he went to sea and plied this trade until 1880 when he came to America. He settled on a farm in Spruce Hill Township, but most of his time was spent in writing and woodcarving. His only tool in making the Bible scenes and the quotations was a jack-knife, besides—of course—a large amount of natural talent and a liberal portion of patience. He is supposed to have received the sum of eighteen dollars for the pulpit. It was purchased by the congregation and installed in the church July 17, 1899. Four years later it was transferred to the new church where it stands, not only as a piece of art, but a worthy candidate for a fireproof museum or archive, where it would not be in danger of being lost.

Mr. Christianson was also a literary man of ability. He has left a large number of essays and stories in manuscript, many of them with original drawings and illustrations. He had the most beautiful and perfect handwriting. He was a born artist. Had he received training and direction of his talents the world would have heard of him.

The Question of Language

The work of the Church was from the very first carried on in the Swedish language and among the Swedes, or at least among the Scandinavians. The word "countrymen (landsmän) occurs very frequently in pastoral, committee and Conference reports, as well as in the church press. The minutes of the Red River Valley Conference were written in the Swedish until 1928, though the reports from the Schools within the Conference were in English from 1919 and on.

In 1882 Pastor P. Sjoblom reported to the Conference the remarkable fact that a girl of American birth and from an unchurched home learned Swedish in order to have an opportunity to receive confirmation instruction.[19]

The church was mindful of the needs of the people in regard to the use of the English language. As early as 1886 a committee of one member from each District was appointed, which committee "shall report to the Conference at its next meeting to what extent the English language is used in our congregations, either in public worship, Sunday School, catechetical instruction or in the parochial school; the committee being accorded the privilege of adding any suggestions growing out of the investigation." [20]

Four years later the official report declares that "whereas the church aims at the salvation of souls and thousands of various nationalities, who confess the Lutheran faith, are lost because they do not have the Word of God preached to them in their own language, it is our duty to do our utmost by the help of God to bring the Gospel to as many as possible." [21] From one community it was reported that "nine business men in the village presented a petition that church work be started there in the English language." [22]

There may have been many instances where the Swedish language was used too long in the church services and particularly in catechetical instruction. The Swedish was to many of the younger people a foreign tongue, and even though they willingly and obediently memorized the catechism and Bible verses, they did not get the full benefit of the instruction. Then, too, the use of any foreign language in a community confined the influence of preaching, teaching and church activities to those who had the advantage of speaking that particular language. The World War I, 1914-1918, turned the foreign language speaking churches more or less toward the language of the land, though it took two decades more to make the change complete, especially as far as the Swedes were concerned.

Churches—In Memoriam

"The memory of them is forgotten."

It is proper that we remember the congregations which "were and are not," which "like the flower of the field" have blossomed forth—though they were but small forget-me-nots—and then faded away. As already noted, the sacrifices and efforts were not in vain, though the congregations are now extinct. The field might have been small and the season brief, but even so sheaves were gathered into the Kingdom of God.

There were reasons and conditions which accounted for the discontinuance of many of these churches.

There were the congregations which were somewhat isolated, which thrived for a while and then pined away, perhaps because the population shifted or modern transportation facilities made it possible to affiliate with larger churches. As an illustration we may mention the Lake Moses congregation organized in 1880 by the Swedes living near Lake Moses, not very far from Evansville, Minn.[23] The congregation considered itself a branch or annex to the Christine Lake church, but the roads were poor and means of travel primitive, so it was considered convenient to have this church closer. In the wintertime the means of travel was "a home-made sled drawn by a couple of steers and the father or the oldest son would walk ahead, leading the steers by a rope."[24] The church building was about eighteen by twenty-eight, with two windows on each side. Seats were planks nailed on blocks of wood. Per Lofdahl made a pulpit and pews during the winter of 1893. The congregation numbered at one time about thirty members. It was disbanded about the year 1911. The church building was sold for lumber and only a cemetery remains on a

Photo courtesy Marian Peterson
Pulpit, Spruce Hill

First Cemetery—Oscar Lake

Site of First Church—Oscar Lake

little hill overgrown with weeds and brush, most of the tombstones being pushed over by irreverent vandals and grazing cattle.[25] Some of the footmarkers on the cemetery indicate tragedy and sorrow in the pioneer home, where a twelve year old and a six year old died the same year (1888) and an eleven year old died the following year—all in the same family.[26]

In 1887 a small "Swedish Lutheran congregation" was organized in Twin Valley, Minnesota. "For a period of nine years the work was at a standstill, but was then revived and the fifteen families were hopeful for the future." [27] In 1907 we read in the minutes of the Central District: "Resolved, that the Lima, Twin Valley, Minnesota, and the church at Rutland, N. D., which have practically ceased to exist, since the people have moved away, be dropped from the Conference Records."[28]

Since the organization of the Conference in 1913 sixteen other congregations in what is now the Red River Conference, have—for one reason or another—disappeared. Most of them have merged with other neighboring congregations of the Augustana Church or other Lutheran groups. But they are worthy of "honorable mention." [29] Eleven congregations have been organized within the Conference during the same period of time.[30]

The Trinity church, Sebeka, Minn., was organized in Paddock, Minn., in 1890, and moved into Sebeka six years later. The congregation at Compton found it difficult to unite on a central location for their church, in spite of the urgings by the District.[31] As a result it had two churches for some time, and there is today a cemetery on the prairie where a monument marks the place where the "Gustava" church once stood.

"What Mean These Stones?"

In the story of Jacob's journey we read that "Rachel died, and was buried in the way of Ephrath," Gen. 35:19. Near the Chatham Square at the Bowery in metropolitan New York is

161

an old Hebrew Cemetery with 153 names of early settlers buried there. The historian who has immortalized this God's Acre, used from 1682 to 1831, calls his book "Portraits Etched in Stone." [32]

Within the territory of the Red River Valley Conference there are many single graves which are not marked by anything but a more or less dilapidated fence and some lilac bushes, many times not even that. These graves usually date back to the time before any congregation was organized, when a member of the family died and was laid to rest in the virgin soil of the homestead. Every such spot causes us to remember the trials and sorrows of pioneer life, where in a special way the poet's words could be applied:

> "Life is real and life is earnest
> And the grave is not its goal."

Some Rachel, perhaps, was buried "in the way."

Then there are larger burial grounds which point to the distant past, shrines which call to mind the question: "What mean these stones?"

We are not in a position to give a detailed and comprehensive history of all such cemeteries, but we shall mention two representative "stones" and sacred places.

First among these is a monument on a hill, one mile north and one mile west of the Oscar Lake church. The inscription reads:

> "1866—In loving memory
> of about 200 of the first settlers
> that are laid to rest here.
> Erected by relatives and friends
> May 30, 1921."

About one-fourth of a mile directly north stands a large boxelder tree which is beginning to suffer from old age. It marks the exact site of the first church building in the Red River Valley Conference. The church was located on the Olof Fahlin homestead a short distance from the present farm buildings.

About two miles northeast of Nelson, Minnesota, stands a monument of polished red granite about fifteen feet high. It was erected in 1912 and marks the site of a cemetery used 1868-1878. "This monument is erected to the memory of the first pioneers and their descendants who are resting in this place. Their names and ages are recorded and sealed under this stone."

Abiding Values

Was there ever a period in human history when events moved more swiftly than during the last quarter of the nineteenth and the first half of the twentieth century, particularly in America, including the great northwest? The pioneers came empty handed, built their homes and primitive churches. Outside of every church in those early days, whether in the town or country, there were long lines of hitching posts where the oxen and horses were tied during the time of the services in church. Or at best there were church barns. The conveyances consisted of buggies and lumber wagons. One woman told the writer that in the pioneer days they kept their new surrey in the shed two years without using it, for fear they would be considered proud, since every one else had simpler vehicles. It took time to go to church in those days—the roads were poor, travel slow, and services long. It was nothing uncommon for confirmands to have to walk fifteen to twenty miles round trip to attend classes.

But there was a definite hunger for the Word of God and for spiritual fellowship. "Wherever the pioneers settled, the ringing of the church bells was a familiar sound and church spires were a familiar sight. . . . The story of the churches begins with humble things—a few devoted people, a pioneer minister or priest, the building of a church." [33]

Now and then there were those who were martyrs. How vividly I remember an old lady whom I visited. She had been married to an unchurched man. He was now dead. She wanted to go to church, but her two grown sons were not interested. (They were later.) She had a charming personality and a radiant faith. "I will have to show you, Pastor, something that I have," she said, going to a drawer and pulling out a little white bundle. Having untied the cloth she took out an old Swedish psalmbook. It had been so well worn that I doubt if there were a dozen leaves still clinging to the binding and every leaf was without margins since they were worn off. "There is hardly a day, but I have read this book. I couldn't get to church, so this psalmbook has been my pastor. I have asked that the book be put with me in my coffin when I am buried." And it was.

Some of the District minutes and pastoral reports tell of special seasons of refreshing. "There have been spiritual times of revivals. . . . The parish has had a special experience of grace in that many have begun to ask in deep sincerity, What shall we do to be saved? As we have conducted catechetical discussions God has led many to clarity and light. The hunger for the Word of God, and the power of that Word has been evident in the many worshipers at our regular services and at the mission meetings." [34] Again says a Conference president: "No one can report any great revivals, but many say that the Lord through his Word has worked mightily among the people, so that many have had their eyes opened, many have found life and peace in the name of the only-begotten Son. Yes, many walk worthily of the Gospel. One pastor has had the great joy of receiving four adults into the church through baptism and confirmation." [35]

We admire the zeal and endurance of the pioneer pastors.

They feared no dangers, eschewed no trials. They were "in labor more abundant. . . . In journeyings often . . . in perils of water . . . in perils of their countrymen . . . in perils in the city . . . in perils in the wilderness . . . in weariness and painfulness, in watchings often, in hunger and thirst . . . in cold and nakedness," 2 Cor 11:26ff.[36]

We also think of the way some of the pastors have presented the cause of the church in their correspondence. Pastor J. O. Cavallin wrote under the caption, "Eko från Norden,"—Echoes from the North, graphic pictures from the mission field, travelogues, etc. Pastor J. B. Sorenson pictured "min lilla vrå bland coulees"—My little Corner among the Coulees—North Dakota. Pastor J. H. Randahl presented his informative and touching home mission reports to the Conference.

The pastors were supported in their labors by many consecrated laymen, who did not only assist in the pulpit ministry, but helped to carry the work of the church in general. The Red River Valley Conference has had a large number of devoted men and women leaders who have marched and led in the army of the Lord. A large number of young people from the congregations of the Conference have entered the direct service of God and the Church as pastors and missionaries.

The modern church presents an altogether different aspect on Sunday morning from the pioneer church, in outward appearance. Around the church are automobiles—many of the latest models—which as a group are worth several times more than the cost of the church and all its furnishings. Yes, even the stone monuments on the church cemetery represent as great a monetary value as the church edifice.

But in the pulpit stands the pastor proclaiming the same eternal Gospel message, pointing to the same Savior as did the pioneer pastors. The congregation still sings the same hymns as of yore. The children—and frequently also adults—

are brought to the same baptismal font to become the children of God and members of the church. When death comes and the earthly tabernacle crumbles into dust in God's Acre—the cemetery—the saved soul is carried by the angels into Paradise. In God's own time the graves shall give up their dead and the militant church shall be the Church Triumphant. Then shall appear the abiding values in the work of the church of Christ—including the pioneers.

"What has been sown in dishonor shall be raised in glory."

References

[1] From Minutes of Larf Congregation, Sweden, 1846.
[2] Ibid, 5/17/1747.
[3] Ibid, 6/2/1762.
[4] Ibid, 5/5/1790.
[5] Ibid, 1820.
[6] God's Kingdom Among the Hills of Eagle Lake, p. 34.   From 1875.
[7] Ibid, p. 34. From 1889.
[8] Ibid, p. 34. From 1890.
[9] Ibid, p. 34. From 1891.
[10] Ibid, p. 34. From 1882.
[11] Constitution and By-laws of Svenska Församlingen i Torsby (Gwinner) p. 15.
[12] Ibid, p. 23.
[13] History of Fahlun Church.
[14] Salol.
[15] Wennersborg.
[16] Minnesalbum, Eagle Lake, 1921.
[17] Minutes, Lake Park Congregation, p. 111.
[18] Minnesalbum, Eagle Lake, 1921.
[19] Minutes, Minnesota Conference, 1882, p. 10.
[20] Ibid, 1886, p. 63.
[21] Ibid, 1890, p. 4.
[22] Ibid, 1907, p. 145.
[23] Klein, K. M. History of Millerville, pp. 9, 11.
This is the story of a Roman Catholic community and the author says: "When the push of the Swedes, 1867, was averted we find a number of Englishmen strewn in, that shall be brought out. We hated neither the Swedes nor the English, but neither had a heart for our religion or language (German). They were not desirable in our colony."
[24] From a Letter by Mr. Albin Beckman, Nelson, Minn., January 2, 1953.
[25] Writes Mr. Beckman: "In the little graveyard is buried John Busse, a German, who donated the lot for the church and the burial hill. He was the first person buried there. The deed to the lots was recorded in 1881, but no doubt the congregation was organized before that."
[26] Again we quote Beckman: "I remember the winter 1887-88 as an outbreak of diphtheria took three of the Hammargren children. The snow was so deep a team could not get through. Some husky men made a large hand sled and pulled the coffins to the graveyard by hand."
[27] Minnesota Stats Tidning, January 8, 1896.   P. P. Hedenstrom.
[28] Minutes Central District, 1907, volume II, p. 62.
[29] They are: Wennersborg, Kensington, Minn., 1871-1948; Fryksände, Evansville, Minn., 1877-1932; Zion, Town of Ward, Clarissa, Minn., 1901-1918; Hishult, Shotley, Minn., 1912-1944; Emanuel, Crookston, Minn., 1886-1922; Fridhem, Cragnes, Fargo, N. Dak., 1898-1923; West Emmaus, Kennedy, Minn., 1896-1951; Nyskoga, Sandville, Minn., 1894-1937; Bloomwood, Argyle, Minn., 1905-1947; Bethania, Badger, Minn., 1899-1941; Newfolden, Minn., 1896-1924; Graceton, Minn., 1921-1941; Spooner, Minn., 1921-1927; Middle River,

Minn., 1910-1915; Maria, Braddock, N. Dak., 1890-1948; Nordskoga, Randen, Minn., 1906-1920.

Note: The Wennersborg congregation united with Bethel, Hoffman. In 1920 it was reported: "In Spooner we have a Sunday School of 60-70 children and at present there is not a single Protestant pastor in Spooner or Baudette." (R.R.V. Conference Minutes, 1920, p. 22.) See also R.R.V. Conference Minutes, 1928, pp. 22-23.

Mt. Carmel bought the Graceton church for $500 and moved it eighteen miles to Willow Creek and the congregations merged. (R.R.V. Conference Minutes, 1942, p. 34.)

The Maria church, Braddock, N. Dak., merged in 1948 with the Zion and Klepp churches (Lutheran Free Church) of Kintyre, N. Dak., to form the Trinity church. (History of First Church, Bismarck, N. Dak. Miss Mabel Olson, in MSS.)

Other congregations which have existed for some time in the territory which is now the R.R.V. Conference are: Bethel, Ray, N.D.; Herman, Alamo, N.D.; Sharon, McGregor, N.D.; Salem, Flasher, N.D.; Saron, Midway, N.D.; First, Fullerton, N.D.; Vasa, Litchville, N.D.; Sophia, Timmer, N.D.

[30] They are: Zion, Alvarado, 1914; First, Hines, 1915; Zion, Leonard, 1916; First, Salol, 1919; First, Miltona, 1921; Immanuel, Swift, 1922; Augustana, Detroit Lakes, 1931; Bethany, Williams, Ebenezer, Roosevelt, 1941; Grace, Browerville, 1944—all in Minnesota; Messiah, Fargo, N.D., 1950.

[31] Minutes, Alexandria District, 1898, p. 124.

[32] New York Times, November 12, 1952.

[33] Blegen, Theodore. Building Minnesota, p. 348, 350.

[34] Newspaper Clippings, Report in Minutes Central District, p. 4.

[35] Minutes, Minnesota Conference, 1888, p. 13.

[36] "It was much harder than before to break away from home. My oldest son wept and asked his father so touchingly not to go away. He wanted to know how long I was going to be away and I did not dare to tell him. My wife had been depressed many days, not to say weeks, in the thought that she was to carry all the worry and responsibility for the home alone. . . . Many people thought me to be calloused and without feeling, and did not notice—even though they were with me those long hours—what intense struggles went on in my inner being." (Skaffaren, Sept. 10, 1890, J. Magney.)

XI. BIBLIOGRAPHY

Minnesskrift, 1858-1908.
Minnesota Konferensen av Evangelisk-Lutherska Augustana Synoden.
Femtioars Jubileum.
Red River Runs North
Vera Kelsey, Harper Brothers, New York. Copyright, 1951.
Svenskarna i Amerika. Historisk skildring i ord och bild av Svenskarnas
underbara öden i U.S. och Canada.
The Religious Aspect of Swedish Immigration.
A Study of Migrant Churches. George M. Stephenson.
Minneapolis. The University of Minnesota Press, 1932.
Ett Minne i Ord och Bild, över den Svenska Evang. Lutherska Red River
församlingen.
Med anledning av 25ars festen den 27 juni, 1901.
Utgiven av församlingen. Pastor L. P. Lundgren.
Minnesota Conferensen och dess församlingar. II Volumes. Dr. Emil Lund.
1926.
De Svenska Lutherska Församlingarnas och Svenskarnas Historia i Amerika.
E. Norelius. II Volumes.
A Church Planted. The Story of the Lutheran Minnesota Conference, 1951-
1876. 1948. Dr. Emeroy Johnson.
Minnesota's Campaign for Immigrants. Theodore C. Blegen.
Fire Upon the Earth.
The Story of the Christian Church. Norman F. Langford. 1949.
The Westminster Press.
Protokollbok for Central Distriktet av Minnesota Konferensen, Vol. I, 1898-
1906, 191 pages. Vol. II, 1906-1910, 176 pages.
Protokollbok for James River Distriktet av Minnesota Konferensen av Evan-
gelisk Lutherska Augustana Synoden. 1898-1944. 164 pages .
Präirieblomman, Augustana Book Concern, Rock Island, Ill.
Korsbaneret, Augustana Book Concern, Rock Island, Ill.
Banbrytaren, S. J. Kronberg. 1906.
Minutes of the Bismarck District. 1916-1940. 296 pages.
Minutes of North Dakota District. 1909-1916. 141 pages.
Minutes of James River District. 1898-1906. 55 pages.
Minutes of Sheyenne District. 1916-1937. 299 pages. 1937-1941, 102 pages.
Bulletin. Swedish Historical Society.
Catalogue, Hope Academy. Augustana College Archives.
Catalogue, Northwestern College, R.R.V. Conference Archives, Alexandria,
Minn.
History of Alexandria District. J. Edor Larson. R.R.V. Conference Minutes.
1930.
Minutes of the Minnesota Conference.
Minutes of the Augustana Synod.
Minutes of the Red River Valley Conference.
Rätta Hemlandet och Augustana.
Ungdomsvännen, Rock Island, Ill.
Skaffaren.
Minnesota Stats Tidning.
Luthersk Kyrkotidning.
Evangelisk Luthersk Tidskrift.
Anniversary Booklets of 32 Congregations of the Red River Valley Confer-
ence published on anniversary occasions. In print or manuscript.

INDEX

169

Hocanzon, L. A., 27, 31, 36, 40, 80, 132 ff.
Hoffman, 67, 70.
Holmberg, P. J., Mrs., 146.
Holmes City, 25, 67, 70.
Holmquist, Alfred, 151.
Holmquist, L. P., 92.
Holmstedt, V. E., 92.
Home Mission, 27, 28, 41, 42, 43, 44, 45, 49, 58, 61, 74.
Hoorn, Arvid, 83.
Hope Academy, 86 ff.
Håfgång, 156.

Idso, Ingham, 146.
Immigrants, 12, 13, 14, 15, 16, 25, 29, 37, 38, 39, 40, 66, 73.

Jackson, Lillie, Sister, 142.
James River District, 75.
Jamestown, 74.
Johnson, Aaron, 99.
Johnson, Alfred, 99.
Johnson, Carl, Mrs., 146.
Johnson, Constant, 63.
Johnson, H. A., 151.
Johnson, J. A., 41.
Johnson, J. W., 99.
Johnson, Louis, 39, 41, 66, 70, 90, 92, 128.
Johnson, Mary, 120.
Johnson, Nels, 99.
Josephson, Sadie, 142.
Junior Missionary Society, 144, 145.
Junior Secretary, 144, 145.

Kansas Conference, 48.
Kassa, O., 67.
Kenmare, 74.
Kennedy, 31, 80, 81.
Kensington, 67.
Kensington Stone, 12, 15.
Kjellgren, Theo., 73, 77.
Kjellin, Bertil, 151.
Kjellin, Edith, 142.
Krantz, J. A., 49, 51, 77, 78.
Kronberg, S. J., 27, 39, 41, 65, 66, 67, 91, 92.
Kulm, 79.

Ladies Aid, 38.
Lagerstrom, J. S., 30.
Lake Ida, 23, 25, 67.
Lake Moses, 160.
Lake Park, 86, 116.
Langsjoen, N. P., 97.
Language, 158, 159.
Larson, Amanda, 123.
Larson, C. H., 110, 116-119.
Larson, Jean, 124.
Larson, J. Edor, 63.
Larson, Otto, 151.
Laymen's Conference, 149, 150, 151.
Lehart, N., 53, 110.
Leonard, 71.
Leonardson, Otto, 150.
Lignite, 76.
Liljedahl, J. E., 77.
Lindahl, Delphine, 144.
Lindberg, C. H., 99.
Lindberg, John, 99.
Lindh, L. O., 66.
Lindholm, S. A., 55, 72, 73, 77, 99.
Lindquist, Lin, 96.
Little Sauk, 67.
Lofdahl, P., 160.
Louisiana Purchase, 11.
Lund Academy, 91.
Lundberg, L. P., 75.
Lundblad, J. P., 17, 65, 66, 67, 81, 127 ff.
Lundgren, Alma, Mrs. 137, 139.
Lundgren, Aug., 99, 116.
Lundgren, L. P., 81, 116, 133.
Lundquist, L. J., 73.
Luther College, 100.
Lutheran Benevolent Society, 88.
Lutheran Bible Institute, 146.
Luther League, 146.

Maddock, 96.
Magney, Jonas, 16, 17, 24, 25, 26, 67, 125 ff.
Mahlberg, P. B., 99.
Malm, Nels, 29.
Maple Sheyenne, 72.
Mariedahl, 128.
Markstrom, A., 37.
Mattson, A., 82, 120.

171

172

Riggers, H., 89.
Roseau, 37, 58, 82, 83.
Rosenquist, Kermit, Mrs., 124.
Rosenthal, Esther, 144.
Runestone, 12.
Rutland, 42, 161.
Ryding, J. S., 120.

Samuelson, C. W., 77.
Sandstead, G. W., 63.
Sauk Center, 18, 19, 23.
School of Nursing, 115.
Sebeka, 67, 161.
Senior Band, 143.
Setterlund, P. P., 92.
Sheyenne, N. D., 59, 74, 76, 78.
Sheyenne District, 60, 62, 76, 146.
Shipp, J. E., 73.
Singing, 156.
Sjoblom, P., 15, 27, 28, 67, 74, 133.
Sjogren, H. L., 147.
Sjostrand, C. E., 100, 103.
Sjostrom, A. F., 14.
Slaughter, 73.
Smellie, W. G., 151.
Smith, H. A., 150, 151.
Solomonson, Carl, 97, 140.
Sorenson, J. B., 165.
Souris, 76.
Soxie, Harry, 141.
Spaeth, A. W., Mrs., 143.
Spangberg, 42.
Spruce Hill, 25, 67, 158.
Standish, G., Mrs., 138, 143.
Stenstrom, L. P., 92, 134 ff.
Stephen, 32, 33, 37, 80, 82.
Stillwater, 53.
St. Hilaire, 80, 82.
St. Paul, 11, 28.
St. Peter, 30.
Sture, N. J., 81.
Strandquist, 81.
Swan Lake, 18.
Sward, J. P., 73.
Sweden, Swedish, 12, 13, 23, 28, 29, 158.
Swenson, J., 29.
Swenson, S. G., 89.
Swenson, S. W., 63, 72, 116, 117.
Swenson, S. W., Mrs., 137, 143.

Sundberg, W., 151.
Sunday School, 144, 156.
Synod, 54, 59.

Tabitha, 82.
Tambling, W. L., 92.
Thief River Falls, 81, 82, 141.
Thirteen Towns, 81.
Tolley, 76.
Travel, 14, 17 ff., 29, 31 ff., 37.
Trial, 43, 68, 73, 74, 77, 78, 165.
Tuleen, N. P., 76, 77.
Turnblad, Alice, 142.
Twin Valley, 161.

Udden, Svante, 41, 74, 81.
Underwood, 76.
Upsala, 25.

Valley City, 42, 74, 76, 77.
Vaughn, Mabel, 92.

Wahlin, A., 65.
Wahlund, G., 101, 140.
Walker, 71.
Wallin, J. A., 116.
Wanneberga, 128.
Warren, 30, 31, 32, 34, 69, 77, 81, 98, 110, 140.
Warroad, 82, 83.
Wartburg Seminary, 89.
Wennersborg, 24, 65, 129.
Werner, E. J., 73.
Westin, A. A., 73.
Westman, John, 99.
White Stone Hill, 42, 67, 69, 76.
Wilton, 76.
Winnipeg, 34, 35.
Women's Missionary Society, 139.

Young, Gustav, 15.
Youngdahl, A. C., 92.
Young People's Mission Band, 143.
Youngquist, J. G., 151.
Young Women's Missionary Society, 143.

Zionsborg, 67.